a c   o r y

WOMEN *in* BRITAIN
1900–2000

Annette Mayer

Hodder & Stoughton

A MEMBER OF THE HODDER HEADLINE GROUP

Acknowledgements

For Iris Haynes

The front cover illustration shows *Ruby Loftus screwing a breech-ring* by Dame Laura Knight, Reproduced courtesy of The Imperial War Museum, London.

The publishers would like to thank the following individuals, institutions and companies for permission to reproduce copyright illustrations in this book: The Advertising Archives, page 111; © Bettmann/Corbis, page 114; Hulton Archive, page 84; The Imperial War Museum, London, page 90; Topham Picturepoint, pages 19, 40, 70; *Woman's Own*, page 68.

The publishers would also like to thank the following for permission to reproduce material in this book: Cambridge University Press for the table from *Women's Work, 1840–1940* by Elizabeth Roberts, Cambridge University Press, 1995; Faber and Faber Ltd for the extract from *The Education of Girls* by John Newsom, Faber and Faber Ltd, 1948; extract from From the Wings by Thelma Cazalet-Keir published by The Bodley Head. Used by permission of The Random House Group Limited; Routledge and Kegan Paul for the extracts from *Britain's Married Women Workers* by Viola Klein, Routledge and Kegan Paul, 1965 and *Women's Two Roles, Home and Work* by Alva Myrdal and Viola Klein, Routledge and Kegan Paul, 1956.

Every effort has been made to trace and acknowledge ownership of copyright. The publishers will be glad to make suitable arrangements with any copyright holders whom it has not been possible to contact.

Orders: please contact Bookpoint Ltd, 130 Milton Park, Abingdon, Oxon OX14 4SB. Telephone (44) 01235 827720, Fax: (44) 01235 400454. Lines are open from 9.00–6.00, Monday to Saturday, with a 24 hour message answering service. Email address: orders@bookpoint.co.uk

British Library Cataloguing in Publication Data
A catalogue record for this title is available from the British Library

ISBN 0 340 780746

First published 2002
Impression number   10 9 8 7 6 5 4 3 2 1
Year   2008 2007 2006 2005 2004 2003 2002

Contents

Preface

To the general reader

Although the *Access to History* series has been designed with the needs of students studying the subject at higher examination levels very much in mind, it also has a great deal to offer the general reader. The main body of the text (i.e. ignoring the 'Study Guides' at the ends of chapters) forms a readable and yet stimulating survey of a coherent topic as studied by historians. However, each author's aim has not merely been to provide a clear explanation of what happened in the past (to interest and inform): it has also been assumed that most readers wish to be stimulated into thinking further about the topic and to form opinions of their own about the significance of the events that are described and discussed (to be challenged). Thus, although no prior knowledge of the topic is expected on the reader's part, she or he is treated as an intelligent and thinking person throughout. The author tends to share ideas and possibilities with the reader, rather than passing on numbers of so-called 'historical truths'.

To the student reader

This title ensures the results of recent research are reflected in the text and includes features aimed at assisting you in your study of the topic at AS Level, A Level and Higher. Two features are designed to assist you during your first reading of a chapter. The *Points to Consider* section following each chapter title is intended to focus your attention on the main theme(s) of the chapter, and the issues box following most section headings alerts you to the question or questions to be dealt with in the section. The *Working on . . .* section at the end of each chapter suggests ways of gaining maximum benefit from the chapter.

There are many ways in which the series can be used by students studying History at a higher level. It will, therefore, be worthwhile thinking about your own study strategy before you start your work on this book. Obviously, your strategy will vary depending on the aim you have in mind, and the time for study that is available to you.

If, for example, you want to acquire a general overview of the topic in the shortest possible time, the following approach will probably be the most effective:

1. Read chapter 1. As you do so, keep in mind the issues raised in the *Points to Consider* section.
2. Read the *Points to Consider* section at the beginning of chapter 2 and decide whether it is necessary for you to read this chapter.
3. If it is, read the chapter, stopping at each heading or sub-heading to note

down the main points that have been made. Often, the best way of doing this is to answer the question(s) posed in the Key Issues boxes.

4. Repeat stage 2 (and stage 3 where appropriate) for all the other chapters.

If, however, your aim is to gain a thorough grasp of the topic, taking however much time is necessary to do so, you may benefit from carrying out the same procedure with each chapter, as follows:

1. Try to read the chapter in one sitting. As you do this, bear in mind any advice given in the *Points to Consider* section.
2. Study the flow diagram at the end of the chapter, ensuring that you understand the general 'shape' of what you have just read.
3. Read the *Working on...* section and decide what further work you need to do on the chapter. In particularly important sections of the book, this is likely to involve reading the chapter a second time and stopping at each heading and sub-heading to think about (and probably to write a summary of) what you have just read.
4. Attempt the *Source-based questions* section. It will sometimes be sufficient to think through your answers, but additional understanding will often be gained by forcing yourself to write them down.

When you have finished the main chapters of the book, study the 'Further Reading' section and decide what additional reading (if any) you will do on the topic.

This book has been designed to help make your studies both enjoyable and successful. If you can think of ways in which this could have been done more effectively, please contact us. In the meantime, we hope that you will gain greatly from your study of History.

Robert Pearce

1 Women in 1900

POINTS TO CONSIDER

The purpose of this chapter is twofold. The first objective is to gain an overview of the political, economic and social status of women at the beginning of the twentieth century. The second is to understand the complex interaction of forces and ideas which were to affect women's progress over the next hundred years. As you read this chapter, identify first the main features relating to women's lives. Then familiarise yourself with the key issues.

1 The Status of Women in Britain, 1900–14

> **KEY ISSUE** What were the main features of women's lives in Britain between 1900 and 1914?

In 1900, as indeed in 1999, Britain was ruled by a female monarch. As a remarkable era drew to a close, Queen Victoria still commanded widespread public support. Her death in 1901 prompted a national display of genuine grief.

Victoria ruled, however, over a society in which her female contemporaries were largely treated as second-class citizens. Women were denied the same political rights as men; in employment they experienced exploitation and low pay, whilst the doors to professional careers remained largely closed. Society expected women to implement their 'natural' duties of wives and mothers and assumed, without question, that women were the economic and social dependants of men. The inequalities they suffered were pervasive. The degree of discrimination and restrictions endured by women both publicly and privately acted as a powerful deterrent, discouraging many women from seeking reforms. It was difficult to break through traditional barriers in order to achieve emancipation. Yet by the end of the century women had undeniably made significant progress in terms of their position within society as exemplified by their participation in politics and greater economic and social independence. In order to appreciate the extent to which women had successfully changed their lives by 2000, it is important to understand first the conditions which affected them in 1900.

a) The Political Status of Women, 1900–14

One question that we should ask is what was the breadth of political influence exercised by women before 1914? How did their influence compare with that of men? The first point to appreciate is that in 1900 women possessed very limited political rights. Single women ratepayers had received the franchise to vote in local elections in 1869, and were granted the right to elect county councillors in 1888. Only in 1894 did married women who were householder occupiers in their own right receive the suffrage in local elections. At a national level, all women were denied the vote whereas the majority of men had the vote after 1884.

Women were excluded from national politics for several reasons. Although a campaign for female suffrage had been active since the second half of the nineteenth century, male politicians had ensured, with monotonous regularity, that any proposed legislation to admit women to the franchise was rejected. The attitudes of politicians, as well as society as a whole, were a major factor in preventing female political equality with men.

Amongst the opponents, anti-suffragists adhered to the premise that politics constituted a male activity, requiring the logic of a male brain. Women were mentally and physically unsuitable, their decisions determined by volatile emotions. Their political views were too unstable for them to think rationally about complex affairs of state. Other opponents maintained what we can now see was a less gender-prejudiced view, but were still reluctant to concede women the vote. Politicians in particular were motivated by political concerns as to whether the extension of the vote to women would undermine the fortunes of their own political party. Liberals and Labour thought that adding women to the vote would favour the Tories as women were considered to be more conservative-minded. The Liberal governments of 1906–14 were particularly fearful that their parliamentary majority might be overturned by the impact of the female vote. Far better, therefore, to grant adult manhood suffrage before making concessions to women. Furthermore if, as indeed seemed the case between 1906 and 1914, more important matters of state predominated, then women's suffrage would have to be postponed.

Other objections focused on the belief that the vote should only be extended to women if it guaranteed sound government. But after 1908 many politicians began to doubt whether women could be trusted with the vote. Although peaceful campaigning by the National Union of Women's Suffrage Societies (NUWSS) for the vote had been conducted since the late nineteenth century, it was the escalation of a more militant campaign by the Women's Social and Political Union (WSPU) after 1908 which alienated potential sympathy. Men, both inside and outside parliament, who had supported the female suffrage, found it increasingly difficult to condone the tactics of the WSPU as a viable means of protest. In their opinion, if middle-class women chose to resort to hysterical and demeaning behaviour as a way of pressurising politicians, there seemed little justification in conceding their demands. Government could not become the victim of blackmail.

The question of suffrage was also contentious amongst women, with a wide range of pro- and anti-suffragist arguments prevailing. For example, since the majority of men had had the vote since 1884, why should women be excluded from what was a natural entitlement within a democracy? Women had long exercised responsibility in education, public health and as owners of property, yet they were prevented from participating in the decision-making process that governed policies. The vote would enable women to affect policy making, especially where issues concerned the welfare of women. Linking the economic welfare of women with political emancipation was one of the contributory factors behind the success of the NUWSS, the second of the suffrage societies, in attracting working-class women's support, especially in northern textile towns. It was part of a wider agenda to bring about wider emancipation.

Many women maintained a more traditional view of their role in society, one in which they accepted that men were the natural rulers whilst their place was in the home. In this respect, they concurred with the belief of male anti-suffragists that women occupied a different sphere from that of men, one in which they were separate but equal. As Jane Lewis observed, 'women's talents were equal but different to men's and that women's essentially domestic skills were better employed in local rather than national politics'.[1] The female anti-suffragists were a vociferous group, well organised and articulate – and somewhat ironically they proved by their very efficiency that women were capable of being successful leaders and managers of other people! The very existence of their strong opinions indicated the depth of division amongst women regarding their precise role in society.

Women's political influence was limited therefore to local politics where some women had the vote. At a national level, a few women who were members of powerful families acted as political hostesses, but within the corridors of power the right to govern was the prerogative solely of men.

b) The Economic Status of Women, 1900–14

In 1900 women's economic role could be defined as one of economic dependency. In terms of the nature of employment, pay and conditions, women were subject to inferior treatment to that of men although for most working-class men work was poorly paid, hours were long and ill-health common. The sexual divisions within society were powerful factors in determining women's economic status and in ensuring that women occupied less-skilled and lower-paid jobs. For most working-class women, work was an obligation, not a source of personal satisfaction, whilst marriage, as Edward Cadbury noted in 1909, was envisaged more as 'an escape from work'[2] than as a chance for personal happiness.

Women were employed extensively in menial jobs in the first two decades of the twentieth century. Domestic service, which had been the major occupation for working-class women throughout the second half of the nineteenth century, continued to attract large numbers, although increasingly women expressed a reluctance to undertake demanding physical work for such long hours. Nevertheless, mothers of young girls still regarded domestic service as a valid position in which to place their daughters as it helped to augment the family income whilst decreasing the number of mouths to be fed.

Many women were employed as homeworkers within their own home. They were paid according to the number of items produced, via a system known as piecework rates. Added to the tedium of child-care and housework might be the task of taking in laundry, child-minding, making matchboxes, dressmaking or jam-making for long hours at home and for very low pay. Nevertheless, even this derisory income was crucial in assisting families to pay for essential items such as clothing, heating, lighting and food. There was little scope for any additional expenditures.

Another group of women who experienced great exploitation were outworkers. Frequently this entailed working in sweated industries such as lace making, paper-box making, chain making or the whole-sale tailoring industry. Work would be contracted out to small groups of workers employed in small workshops or factories. These industries were too small to warrant the existence of trade unions, so workers were easy victims of long hours and low wage policies. Only in 1909, with the passing of the Trades Act, did a minimum wage begin to operate in these industries.

One perceptible trend before the First World War was the gradual shift towards the employment of women in shop work and clerical jobs. The retail industry expanded appreciably as new department stores opened and small family businesses declined. The work was considered superior to that of domestic work, although the fact that governments felt it necessary to legislate in order to restrict hours of shop work – the 1913 Shop Act limited hours of work to 64 hours per week – indicates that even here there was the potential for exploiting a female workforce.

The other significant area of expansion was in clerical and office work. By 1914, 20 per cent of all clerical workers were women, although women tended to dominate the unskilled and lower paid jobs. Nevertheless, such jobs were clearly more prestigious than many manual occupations.

Whatever the nature of employment, for most working-class women work was a financial necessity in order to avoid the degradation of poverty. Many working-class families lacked a secure, regular income because menial jobs were often seasonal and subject to periods of unemployment. Two reports, one by Charles Booth, *Life and Labour of the London Poor* (1889–1902), and the other by Seebohm Rowntree, *Poverty: A Study of Town Life* (1901), investigated the effects of poverty in London and York in which both noted that women struggled to earn enough money to provide the basic essentials of family life. In general, though, once they were married women would remain at home if they could afford it.

Percentage of women, at different ages, in employment in 1901[3]		
15–34	**35–44**	**45–59**
77%	13%	11%

The overwhelming impression of the economic status of women prior to 1914 was one of inferiority. Men feared that women constituted unwelcome competition in the workplace, and that by working, women would depress men's wages. Women likewise deferred to the belief that the man should be the main breadwinner, therefore automatically they should earn less than men. Before the First World War female teachers earned 25 per cent less than their male counterparts, as did women civil service clerks, whilst women shop assistants earned about 65 per cent as much as men, despite doing the same work. This was a familiar pattern in industry too, a situation reinforced by attitudes of trade unionists who would resist efforts to grant women parity with men. As a result, women were relegated to the less skilled and lower paid jobs in terms of wage, not least because men felt it unnecessary to train women when they were likely to leave the workforce once they were married. There was a strong incentive for men to protect their crafts and skills especially during times of economic depression. They did not want their jobs further jeopardised by a lower-paid and cheaper work force.

For middle-class women, the opportunities to work were sparse. Men controlled the entry to professions and so imposed barriers to female training and employment. Even in a profession such as teaching, where by 1914 75 per cent of all elementary school teachers were female, few women gained promotion and, once married, dismissal was automatic.

Middle-class women were also deterred by the prevailing attitude, common to men and women of all backgrounds, that a respectable woman's place was in the home. Many opted to do voluntary work, but most subscribed to the popular ideology that their vocation lay in motherhood. Some women had successfully embarked on careers which, in 1800, would have been impossible to pursue, but they were invariably single and often the target of adverse comment by those who felt that such women were suppressing their natural womanly virtues. As yet, therefore, it was still a minority of women who viewed economic dependency on men as degrading.

c) The Social Status of Women, 1900–14

In 1900, a combination of customs, traditional attitudes, and a male-dominated culture determined the social status of women in Britain. The position of the woman within the family unit was merely a micro-cosm of women's position within society as a whole. At both levels women were subordinate to men, their prime duty being domestic rather than public. The most obvious expectation was that women would carry out the duties of wives and mothers, an attitude which had existed for centuries. There were exceptions in that some women, through strength of character and natural ability, did domi-nate their families but they remained in a minority.

However, by the early years of the twentieth century a new factor, namely that of state intervention, gave fresh emphasis to the concept that women had a predominantly maternal role in society. This devel-opment was associated with the philosophy of New Liberalism, which advocated limited State intervention to promote people's welfare. The concern within the government was to improve women's under-standing of the requirements of motherhood on the grounds that this would enable women to carry out their responsibilities more effec-tively.

Several motives influenced this policy. For example, it was clear that working-class women were caught in a cycle of poverty, ill-health, overwork, excessive child-bearing, lack of proper nourish-ment and an ignorance of preventative measures such as household cleanliness. If girls could be educated more effectively for their future duties as mothers, then infant mortality could be greatly reduced and women's health in general would improve. Other, more moralistic thinking also supported this approach. At the beginning of the twentieth century, a number of scientists and soci-ologists were interested in the science of eugenics, of improving racial quality through selective breeding. They believed that pov-erty, ignorance and disease prevailed partly because women had not been adequately educated to understand the principles of good child-rearing and general health care. The improved health of the British race was deemed to be of great national importance. As was evident during the First World War, a strong, healthy nation was an essential prerequisite to the pursuit of an imperialistic foreign policy.

Pressure for greater state provision also emanated from working-class women themselves as they became more vociferous. The long-term impact of universal education resulted in a greater level of political and social awareness amongst women. Through such organ-isations as the Women's Co-operative Guild, views were gathered on the relentless effect of poverty on the lives of working-class women. A collection of letters from working-class members was published by the Guild in 1915. The theme behind many of the letters was that state assistance was now essential in order to alleviate the lives of mothers. It was the duty of the country

> ... to relieve motherhood of its burden, to spread the knowledge of mothercraft that is so often lacking, to make medical aid available when it is needed, to watch over the health of the infant. And since this is the duty of the community, it is also the duty of the State.[4]

The scarcity of any state welfare provision, especially in terms of health-care, clearly heightened women's problems. Women would often endanger or neglect problems of ill health because they could not afford doctors' fees. In addition, ignorance of how to avoid exacerbating complications during pregnancy would lead to long-term medical problems. Childbirth itself could be a very traumatic experience because there was inadequate pain relief. Women would frequently work long hours right up to their confinement and would return to work before they were suitably fit. Few working-class women could afford to pay for a qualified midwife. The trials of pregnancy and childbirth were graphically depicted in the letters from the Women's Co-operative Guild.

> 1 ... how I managed to get through my second confinement I cannot tell anyone. I had to work at laundry work from morning to night, nurse a sick husband, and take care of my child three and a half years old. In addition I had to provide for my coming confinement, which meant that
> 5 I had to do without common necessities to provide doctor's fees, which so undermined my health that when my baby was born I nearly lost my life, the doctor said through want of nourishment. ...
>
> I had to depend on my neighbours for what help they could give during labour and the lying-in period. They did their best, but from the second
> 10 day I had to have my other child with me, undress him and see to all his wants, and was often left six hours without a bite of food, the fire out and no light, the time January, and snow had lain on the ground two weeks.[5]

Poor housing conditions added to the burden of working-class life. Maintaining a degree of cleanliness was a struggle when there were no electric or gas water heaters. The absence of a private bathroom had particular significance. In addition to widespread ignorance about birth control, the lack of privacy within a two or three-roomed house discouraged many women from attempting to use female methods of birth control such as rubber cervical caps.

Female sexuality was viewed very differently in 1900 than it is today. Working-class women hoped that they would find a good husband, but the man's ability to make sound economic provision carried greater weight than his sexual attraction. The notion that women possessed sexual drive and should be equal partners in a sexual relationship was rarely entertained. As a result, women often accepted a submissive, non-demonstrative role within marriage.

Middle-class women were fortunate to avoid the relentless effects of poverty suffered by working-class women. They could usually rely upon greater economic security and independence. The Married Women's Property Acts had helped to liberate women from total economic subordination to their husbands by first, in 1870 granting married women the right to retain personal earnings and personal property and then, in 1882, they were entitled to own property in their own right. This had important implications in that, unlike working-class women, those in the middle classes could aspire to a marriage based on love not finance.

Nevertheless, middle-class women still shared many of the problems encountered by their working-class counterparts. Society disapproved of women undertaking paid employment as that would detract from their true vocation in life, motherhood. Writers such as Elizabeth Sloan Chesser idolised motherhood: 'Nothing in the world is so sacred as parenthood and every girl should think and speak of motherhood as one of the holiest things in life.'[6] However, little advice was available to middle-class women on managing or limiting the size of families. Ignorance of birth control and a belief in feminine passivity were as common amongst middle-class as it was amongst working-class women. Before 1918, when Marie Stopes published her book, *Married Love*, it was virtually impossible to obtain any information about birth control. Even amongst early twentieth-century feminists, opinion favoured the importance of motherhood rather than the rights of women to any sexual pleasure.

As in politics, women had to defer to men. Their authority both publicly and privately meant that women had a very defined but limited status within society. This is not to deny that some women had had a distinct impact on Edwardian society – the Pankhurst women who had led and dominated the WSPU were just one prominent example – but most people still concurred with the view that women were the weaker sex.

2 The Key Factors

> **KEY ISSUE** What were the key factors which influenced the far-reaching changes experienced by women during the twentieth century?

This book will seek to identify and analyse the forces which not only swayed society's perception of women but also induced women themselves to engage in new responsibilities, adopt new attitudes and alter the structure of their lives. These forces could be identified as the effects of two world wars, political reform, economic and social progress, technological change, expansion in education, and the emergence of new philosophical ideas. These different causal factors, whether long-term, short-term, political, economic, social or cultural, contributed throughout the century to an on-going process of change. At times this was dramatic, elsewhere barely perceptible. The cumulative effect, however, was substantial.

a) The World Wars

Although Britain found itself at war several times during the twentieth century, it was the two world wars which undeniably had the most decisive impact on the lives of women. However, how can we evaluate the significance of the wars? Economically, women played an essential role, both in 1914–18 and in 1939–45, in alleviating the problems of a depleted workforce. In addition, women discovered a greater degree of individual freedom as conventional attitudes towards social behaviour were weakened. In some respects the wars were a catalyst for extensive reform. It was no mere coincidence that women were granted the franchise at the conclusion of the First World War. Yet a fundamental question that will be subsequently explored is to what extent did the two wars act as a watershed for women? Could it be argued that the wars brought on the whole only short-term emancipation, and that the gains were ultimately less obvious and more long-term?

b) Political Reform

Political reform was also an integral factor in influencing the gradual process of change for women. What were the main acts of political reform and how important were they in improving the political status of women? For example, political emancipation in 1918 and 1928 undoubtedly released enormous opportunities for women. Part of the ensuing discussion, however, will be to examine closely the degree of influence which emancipation accorded women. A number of pertinent questions will need to be answered such as why did so few women enter the national political arena? Were more women attracted to local politics? Was their inability to reverse male domination of politics due as much to women themselves as the male attitudes which they sought to challenge?

c) Economic and Social Progress

Once political emancipation had been attained, the main focus for women campaigners was in the field of economics. One theory to be investigated, therefore, is whether the pace of economic change can be correlated with a greater public profile for women. To what extent were important acts such as the Equal Pay Act (1970) and the Employment Protection Act (1975) the result of pressure from women activists, or were these acts also a response to long-term changes in attitudes to, and expectations of, women? Despite specific legislation, major changes in patterns of employment were not always immediately apparent, although new trends did materialise which in the long-term transformed the position of women in society. For example, one of the effects of technological change was to create new jobs for women in light industry as well as in offices. But were women's lives significantly improved when they were invariably designated to the routine, tedious and less-skilled jobs? A more difficult issue to evaluate, though, is the extent to which women's lives actually improved as a result of wider employment opportunities.

Another area in which legislation has facilitated change for women has been in the field of social reform. Welfare State legislation, based on William Beveridge's report of 1942, was introduced via the 1946 National Insurance Act. Yet the terms of the Act appeared in many respects to be distinctly anti-feminist in that they encouraged a return to domesticity, especially for married women. They were regarded as dependants of their husbands, and could only claim benefits under the 1946 National Insurance Act in conjunction with a claim from their husband. On the other hand, the introduction of family allowances and maternity benefit provided a vital chance for women to escape from the threat of poverty. In 1948, the National Health Service was established, creating for the first time a universal system of health care which could benefit all women. The expansion of the Welfare State was a vital prerequisite in assisting women to challenge their status as second-class citizens. They were no longer so confined by the effects of poverty

Another pertinent question to pursue is whether there was a distinct correlation between the enactment of legislation such as the Sex Discrimination Act (1975), which was designed to redress discrimination, and women's own growth in personal assertiveness which led them to challenge inequality. It is important to appreciate that, as with the acquisition of political equality, social and economic equality for women has been a lengthy process. Legislation does not reverse deeply entrenched attitudes overnight. Nevertheless, such legislation has been crucial in changing the pattern of women's lives.

Legislation was not the only instrument of change. Women's lives were intrinsically affected by shifting attitudes and values and their behaviour adjusted accordingly. Important issues to evaluate will be how women developed different attitudes towards marriage and the family. Also, at what point did women begin to appreciate that, like men, they too had a right to an identity which went beyond that of a predominantly private and domestic identity?

d) Technological Change

The on-going effects of technological change on women's lives have been as dramatic in the twentieth century as they were in the nineteenth. How can we measure these improvements? Have advances in technology been as dramatic on the domestic front as in the workplace in changing women's lives? It could be argued, for example, that whilst technology has revolutionised the lives of both men and women, the effect on women has been far more extensive. Within the home, technology has removed so much of the drudgery from women's daily routine. The task of cooking takes on a new perspective when, instead of having to clean out ashes and re-light a rayburn stove with fresh coal, instant heat can be gained with the flick of a switch. Cleaning a house becomes physically less arduous when the broom is replaced by a vacuum cleaner. A valid question to pursue, however, as the developments of the twentieth century are analysed, is whether technology always brought positive benefits for women. Did the introduction of electrical appliances add pressure on women to produce spotless homes? Did the consequent loss of domestic servants, as young women were drawn into office work and factories, reduce some women's independence within the home as they took on more domestic responsibility? What have been the positive and negative benefits of greater technology in the workplace for women?

e) Education

Another issue to explore is the manner in which changing educational policies have enhanced women's ability to determine their future life-style. As will be seen in subsequent chapters, repeated governments viewed the education of women in a very conservative light, placing considerable emphasis on training women for motherhood and domesticity. Nevertheless, the effects of expanding opportunities in education, especially as higher education became more widely available, must not be underestimated. An articulate, well-educated cohort of women would not forever defer to a male-dominated society, as the explosion of feminist movements in the 1970s demonstrated. How successful, therefore, has education been in reconstructing women's lives during the twentieth century? Can a close correlation be established, for example, between women's success in gaining better jobs and a more innovative education policy?

f) Philosophy

Throughout the twentieth century, the emergence of new philosophical ideas was instrumental in transforming women's role within society. How important were these ideas? The growth of feminist thought during the twentieth century arguably had enormous ramifications for the status of women. This in turn encouraged women not only to question their role in society but also to re-examine historians' methods of analysing twentieth-century history. Mainstream general history had been interpreted very much from a male perspective, neglecting female achievements and contributions. As women became more conscious of the inequalities they endured due to their sex, so they challenged the predominantly male view of history.

The link between historical developments and historical thought was strong. Between 1920 and the early 1960s, the women's movement was weak, unable or unwilling to counteract the popular view of women as domestic creatures. One school of thought, the more radical of two factions, argued that women should be able to compete with men on equal terms whilst the more moderate 'welfare feminists' claimed that women had different needs which required specific legislation. The proliferation of feminist movements from the late 1960s onwards, however, inspired female historians to evaluate the past with a different set of criteria. Some deployed principles of radical politics, such as Marxist ideas, to feminist thought. Emphasis was placed on the extent to which men had exploited women during the emergence of a capitalist society. Other women, known as radical feminists, were more attracted to the agenda of sexual politics in which a patriarchal society was now condemned for its control over women. A further school of thought owed its inception to those within the women's movement who believed that women's past difficulties and failures within society derived from social conditioning. Gender divisions dominated all aspects of public and private life, thus generating an inferior status for women. The process of revision is ongoing. As each new generation of women seeks to define their role in society, so new concepts and beliefs influence their evaluation of the past. They also provide us with fresh observations as to what influenced the changing role of women during the twentieth century.

Having clarified what should be regarded as the main factors which affected the changing status of women during the twentieth century, we should now be in a position to evaluate these issues in subsequent chapters. As each issue is addressed, clear criteria will need to be established by which to compare and contrast the position of women during any one period of time. As the impact and significance of each influence emerges, a more explicit and insightful picture should develop of how and why the status of women in British society changed during the course of the twentieth century.

References

1   Jane Lewis, *Women in England 1870–1950: Sexual Divisions and Social Change* (Wheatsheaf Books Ltd, 1984), xii.
2   Elizabeth Roberts, *Women's Work 1840–1940* (Cambridge University Press, 1995), p. 6.
3   Roberts, *Women's Work*, p. 13.
4   The Women's Co-Operative Guild, *Maternity Letters from Working-Women*, preface by The Right Hon. Herbert Samuel, M.P (G. Bell & Sons, Ltd, 1915), vii.
5   *Ibid.*, p. 24.
6   Elizabeth Sloan Chesser, *From Girlhood to Womanhood* (Cassell & Company, 1913), p. 23.

Summary Diagram
Women in 1900

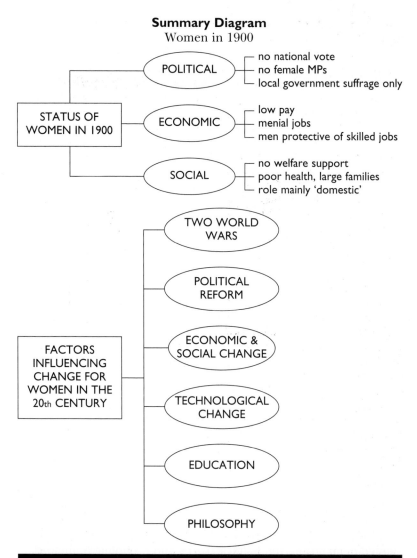

STATUS OF WOMEN IN 1900

POLITICAL
- no national vote
- no female MPs
- local government suffrage only

ECONOMIC
- low pay
- menial jobs
- men protective of skilled jobs

SOCIAL
- no welfare support
- poor health, large families
- role mainly 'domestic'

FACTORS INFLUENCING CHANGE FOR WOMEN IN THE 20th CENTURY

- TWO WORLD WARS
- POLITICAL REFORM
- ECONOMIC & SOCIAL CHANGE
- TECHNOLOGICAL CHANGE
- EDUCATION
- PHILOSOPHY

Working on Chapter 1

At this stage, your main task is to write some brief notes which will then act as reference points when studying subsequent chapters. In order to make valid assessments on how and why women's lives changed during the twentieth century, return to the first section and under the three broad headings of *political, economic* and *social*, note the main features of women's lives and *why* such conditions prevailed. Second, examine the Key Factors and write down two or three questions that would be appropriate to pursue as you read the rest of the book.

2 The First World War, 1914–18

POINTS TO CONSIDER

The First World War was responsible for enormous changes in women's lives. During your first reading of this chapter, you should aim to identify the main economic, political and social factors that affected women. Try and gain an overall impression as to whether these changes were likely to be permanent or not.

KEY DATES

1914	4 August	Britain declared war against Germany.
	7 August	Amnesty for all imprisoned suffragettes.
1915	May	Prime Minister Asquith formed a coalition government.
	June	Ministry of Munitions established.
		NUWSS voted to support war relief work.
	17 July	'Right to Work' march in London.
	July	Munitions Act passed.
		Women's International League for Peace and Freedom established
1916	2 Feb	Conscription introduced for unmarried men.
	June	Conscription extended to married men.
		Speakers' Conference to examine franchise reform set up.
	Dec	Lloyd George became Prime Minister.
1918		Representation of the People Act granted votes to women over the age of 30.
		Maternity and Child Welfare Act passed.
	11 Nov	Armistice with Germany signed.

1 Introduction

The outbreak of war against Germany in August 1914 placed unprecedented demands on the political, social and economic framework of Britain. As the army became engaged in a large-scale war of attrition, so the country was mobilised to extraordinary levels. The war touched people's lives directly, whether it was through work, the task of daily survival or, as the war memorials in every town and village bear testament, the loss of menfolk in so many families. Few could have predicted either the long-term or short-term effects of war, especially when people anticipated the defeat of Germany by Christmas 1914. Four years later, it was clear that pre-war Edwardian society had met its demise. A new agenda determined the nature of society by the beginning of the 1920s.

To what extent, though, did the war transform the lives of women in either the short-term or long-term? As was demonstrated in Chapter 1, numerous factors had constrained the lives of women at the beginning of the century. Women's roles had traditionally been prescribed by a male-dominated society. Economically, women were exploited. Politically, a limited number of women voted in local elections, the rest had no political voice at all. Socially, the majority of women were still expected to be submissive within both their public and private lives. Yet with the outbreak of war, women were drawn into doing 'men's' work, both industrial and agricultural; their circumstances forced them to take on family responsibilities. By the end of the war, some women had gained the vote. Furthermore, many women had experienced much greater personal independence. But how far were these changes purely expedient measures, and therefore only short-term? Or was it the case that as society adjusted to the changing status of women, so more permanent foundations for future social, economic and political progress were established? Three key areas – the level of economic emancipation experienced by women, the reasons for the enfranchisement of women in 1918 and the extent of social change experienced by women – provide insight into understanding how women were affected by the First World War.

2 Economic Emancipation

> **KEY ISSUES** How successful were women in altering their economic status during the war? In what ways were conventional attitudes towards the role of the woman in the workplace challenged?

a) The Realities of War: Unemployment and the 'Right to Work'

In 1911, approximately 4.8 million women were working, the two main occupational groups being first domestic service, then textiles and clothing. However, the declaration of war did not augur well for women's employment. The immediate response within many industries was to contract their female workforce as they anticipated a trade decline and the need to economise. In Lancashire, where the cotton trade relied on imports of raw cotton, supplies were interrupted and female workers were made redundant. Another extensive source of employment for women, domestic service, was badly hit as upper- and middle-class households sought to economise. Traditional female trades, such as fish-gutting and tailoring, also suffered redundancies. By September 1914, some 190,000 women had lost their jobs.

The only areas of expansion for female employment were in clerical and shop work, and then in those industries supplying clothing for the army. The extent of female unemployment, however, prompted the introduction of measures to mitigate some of its worst effects. Queen Mary established The Queen's Work for Women Fund, under the auspices of the Central Committee for Women's Employment, to relieve distress caused by unemployment. Model workrooms opened in Bethnal Green and Stepney where girls from a range of back-grounds – shorthand typists, machinists in blouse factories, workers in cigarette factories and charwomen – were given relief work. They worked a 40 hour week, for threepence (3d) a day, with dinner and tea provided, and were taught new trades, such as needlework and cradle making. Most of the output was for the army – shirts, flannel body belts and socks, all of which were sold at low prices in order not to compete with the established trades.

It was not until 1915 that industries such as munitions began to experience shortages in labour, aggravated by the enlistment of skilled workers. Both government and employers looked to women as an immediate, but short-term, solution to the problem of producing sufficient supplies for the military. Within months, the government appreciated that this potential new labour force would have to be organised efficiently. Hence by the summer of 1915 the government had introduced a Women's War Register with the purpose of investi-gating the availability of women's labour, either trained or untrained. Within two weeks, 33,000 women had enrolled. The readiness of women to work was also illustrated by 'The Right to Work' march organised by the suffrage societies in which 30,000 women marched in London on 17 July 1915, demanding the right to work so that men could enlist for the army. Thus within a year of war commencing, a much more positive attitude towards the employment of women had begun to emerge.

b) The Response of Women: Voluntary Work

The declaration of war prompted a huge wave of patriotic fervour throughout Britain. Whilst men enlisted in the army, women sought to join voluntary organisations aiding the war, a move which was vig-orously endorsed by the suffrage societies, in particular the Women's Social and Political Union (WSPU) led by Mrs. Pankhurst who now ordered a cessation of all suffrage campaigning on the grounds that energies should be transferred to the task of useful war work. Middle- and upper-class women especially regarded voluntary work as a visible and morally righteous way to demonstrate patriotism and support for their menfolk. As with paid work, however, voluntary work provided a significant vehicle by which women could exercise responsibility and thereby refute the male perception that women possessed neither management nor organisational skills.

The accompanying table illustrates some of the women's voluntary organisations which were established during the war.

First World War Women's Voluntary Organisations
  i) Women's Army Auxiliary Corps (WAAC) – provided cooks, clerical workers and drivers for the army. Around 40,000 had joined by November 1918.
  ii) Women's Royal Naval Service (WRNS) – volunteers worked as cooks, waitresses, telegraphists, decoders and in intelligence.
  iii) Volunteer Auxiliary Detachment (VAD) – volunteer nurses who helped to run hospital ships and hospitals in France and England.
  iv) The Women's Land Service Corps (February 1916) and later, the Land Army (1917) – middle-class women (some 23,000 in total) undertook general farm work, to assist in increasing food production which had been hit by German blockades.
  v) Scottish Women's Hospitals – set up by Dr. Elsie Inglis in September 1914 – sent hospital units to work with the French, Belgian, Russian and Serbian armies.

Other upper- and middle-class women responded to the government's call for workers in the munitions factories by volunteering to become one of 'Lloyd George's Munition Girls'. Unlike their working-class contemporaries, they enlisted primarily out of a sense of patriotism rather than the need for a weekly wage. One such volunteer, Monica Cosens, noted that pride was one factor in sending her to the recruitment office.

1 How will you answer your children when they ask what *you* did for the
   Great War? ... I must admit although my heart was bursting with patriotism, there was also a thrill behind it that I was out for adventure, that
   I was about to face things I had never faced before. I was going to put
5 myself to the test as to whether I was fit to serve my country from the
   point of view of intelligence, for it would entail handling a machine, and
   I funked anything to do with machinery ... 1

The employment of middle-class volunteers alongside working-class women could be problematic. The more educated women were often appointed as forewomen and overseers causing suspicion amongst working-class women that they were being spied on, their behaviour the subject of criticism and reproach. An unspoken, but nevertheless common attitude amongst many people was that working-class girls were more vulgar, irresponsible and less interested in their work. It was no mere coincidence that it was older, married women, rather than the young 'munitionettes', who got the vote in 1918.

c) State Mobilisation: Your Country Needs You

As labour shortages became more acute, so there was an influx of women into industry, the largest contingent going into the chemical and engineering industries, followed by banking, the civil service and clerical work. Increasingly women proved very versatile, undertaking numerous 'male' jobs such as working as conductors and drivers on buses and trams. Women were also employed on the railways, although they were denied the excitement of becoming train drivers. Delivering mail and driving the horse-drawn vans for the Royal Mail proved another lure, despite the view amongst both sexes that it was not 'women's' work. Banking and clerical work experienced large increases in female employment, although the majority were only assigned to mundane clerical jobs.

In industry especially, women confounded existing attitudes regarding their work capabilities. Previously, it was assumed that women could only perform less skilled, repetitive jobs like making match boxes. However, as the war progressed, jobs such as gasfitters, crane drivers and plumbers ceased to be the preserve of men alone. In shipbuilding, women were employed as welders, fitters and electricians alongside men, although female supervisors ensured that the two sexes were segregated. But it was the munitions industry that benefited most from female labour. One of the largest factories to employ women was the Woolwich Arsenal. In 1914, it only employed 125 women. By 1917, 25,000 women worked there. [2]

Initially women were assigned to repetition work because of men's anxieties to protect their skilled jobs, but as demand for higher output increased the government was compelled to seek agreements and compromises both with employers and trade unions (see Section 1d). Consequently, complex, skilled jobs were split up into several different operations. Whereas one man might have finished and turned a shell, two women would perform the same task. This separation of tasks was known as the 'dilution' of labour and was a significant compromise by which women were allowed to undertake semi-skilled work. As the illustration on page 19 suggests, women were deemed most suitable for work such as 'turning', 'milling', 'grinding' and filling shells, boring, monotonous jobs which required dexterity but little skill. The most dangerous work was in the filling factories where contact with explosives, TNT, resulted in stained hands and coppery hair.

As the war progressed, the government increasingly appreciated the need to deploy more women in industry. In June 1915, the government founded the Ministry of Munitions and, under its auspices, training centres for factory workers were established throughout the country. At these centres, women learnt to do precision work such as lens and prism making for optical instruments, telescopes and periscopes, and gauge-making for fuses where measurements had to be exact to within a 3/10000 parts of an inch. The assembling of fuses was one of the most prized jobs because perfection was needed at all times.

The decision to introduce conscription in January 1916 placed renewed strains on industry, depriving it of valued skilled male

Turning the outside and forming the Nose-end of a
9.2 inch high-explosive shell

labour. Under the Substitution Scheme of 1916, more women transferred to skilled jobs in order to compensate for the shortage of
labour. As a result, whereas in July 1914, 3,276,000 women were
employed in industry (excluding homeworkers, those in small workshops and the self-employed), by April 1918, 4,808,000 women were
part of the industrial labour force, an increase of about one and a half
million. This mobilisation of the female workforce was unprecedented. Women had defied people's expectations by successfully
demonstrating that they had the stamina, skill and determination to
do men's jobs. The key question was whether they had also achieved
a permanent shift in attitudes towards the role of women in the workplace or whether they were only tolerated as a pragmatic solution to
a short-term problem.

d) Women in the Workplace: Policies and Attitudes

The most contentious issue regarding the employment of women
during the First World War was that of their status and wages. The
government had to solve the problem of integrating women into the
workforce without undermining the formal relationship between
trade unions and employers. Trade unions were particularly concerned to protect their conditions of employment, to ensure that

their skilled jobs were not undermined as the employment of unskilled female labour increased. But the government knew it had to improve industrial output so some compromise, whereby terms of employment were re-defined, had to be reached.

Under various agreements between government, employers and trade unions, the employment of women was permitted, with trade unions agreeing to the dilution of labour. The implications of these negotiations were numerous. First, state intervention in industrial relations had become essential in order to secure co-operation between employers and employees. Voluntary agreements were no longer sufficient. Instead, state intervention became essential.

The second important outcome of the various agreements was that, as women infiltrated the male work area, so employers, trade unions and the government had to re-evaluate their attitudes towards women. Their reactions were mixed. Government propaganda stressed the positive benefits of employing women in an effort to encourage adaptability amongst employers. Yet deep-set prejudice remained. Trade unions such as the Amalgamated Society of Engineers refused to permit female membership because of the implied threat to their own livelihoods. Critics claimed that women were inefficient, making costly mistakes on the production line. Employers pointed to the fact that married women were far more likely to have time off work, whether for sickness, childcare or household tasks such as the weekly washing. Complaints from employers to the Ministry of Reconstruction's Committee on Women in Industry referred to inferior output, poor time-keeping, and lack of initiative.

The issue of whether women should receive equal pay for equal work proved most divisive. In both industrial and non-industrial work, women received lower pay than men and they lacked the industrial muscle with which to fight this discrimination. Within the munitions industry, employers could exploit women by only allocating them to part of a skilled job. Wages were therefore lower on the premise that the job was no longer defined as a skilled job. Thus a skilled job of manning a lathe was reduced from a man's rate of pay of 10 ¾d (about 4 new pence) an hour to a new rate of 5 ¼d (2 new pence) an hour. Employers also circumnavigated the difficult issue of wages by paying women according to piece-rates. The main controversy occurred where women did perform the same skilled jobs as men. Although government circulars stipulated that there should be equal pay for equal work, in practice this became impossible to enforce.

The disagreements between women, employers, trade unions and the government over pay rates persisted until the end of the war. The question of equal pay was to become one of women's key demands in the post-war period. Their experiences of wartime employment clearly highlighted the injustices of pay differentials and gave women an incentive to seek further reform.

e) Conclusion: a 'pyrrhic' victory?

In many respects, the war acted as a facilitator for economic change for women. A key development was the fact that the role of women in the nation's economy was publicly discussed. Government, employers and trade unions were compelled to recognise that women were essential contributors to the war effort. In making this admission, they had at least to set aside the typically male perspective that a woman's place was in the home. Nor could the government afford to be begrudging. Propaganda books, such as Gilbert Stone's *Women War Workers* (1917), were designed to inspire women to support the war effort and to make the necessary sacrifices.

> Stained hands and coppery hair – what are these? Do we fear temporary disfigurement when men, for the same cause, are facing death and the horrible and permanent disfigurement of maimed limbs or blinded eyes?[3]

Women suffragists capitalised on their new-found economic responsibilities and readiness to defend their country. Newspapers such as *The Common Cause* published by the NUWSS (see page 2) regularly praised women for their adaptability to men's work as well as campaigning for equal pay.

> 1 Lincolnshire farmers have hitherto been very sceptical as to the possibilities of utilising women's labour, but after witnessing a dozen women and girls ploughing a straight furrow under exceptionally heavy conditions over the rain-soaked fields, were bound to admit that they did
> 5 their work as well as the average ploughman ... Onlookers were amazed at the ease and dexterity with which they performed their task.[4]

The very positive tone of the article reflected an increasing confidence amongst women that the government would be forced to grant women political rights now that they had undertaken such vital work during the war.

Not all women were converted to the idea that they, alongside men, had an equal right to employment. Traditionalists were reluctant to deprive men of jobs on the basis that it would be demeaning for a man if only the wife worked. The view that women were usually inferior workers, often only working temporarily outside the home, had been instilled in women since the Industrial Revolution. Such attitudes would not necessarily change just because of the exceptional circumstances caused by war.

It is questionable, therefore, whether women gained any significant long-term advantages from their war experiences. Certainly, all the agreements with employers and trade unions had emphasised the importance of reinstating men to their jobs once the war ended. Despite the expectation of suffragists that war must have changed men's opinions of women and that women would be able to maintain permanent jobs in skilled occupations, the demobilisation of women from war-time work after 1918 was substantial (see page 55–6). As Minister of Munitions, Lloyd George's definition of women's future role in society was unambiguous, 'The workers of today are the mothers of tomorrow. In a war of workshops the women of Britain were needed to save Britain; it was for Britain to protect them'.[5] For many women, therefore, wartime economic independence was short-lived, as post-war government policies encouraged women to return to their domestic responsibilities.

3 Political Hurdles

> **KEY ISSUES** Why was the 1918 Representation of the People's Act, which granted limited women's suffrage, passed? Did the actions of the suffrage movement during the war in any way influence the change of opinion which preceded the Act or were other factors more significant in effecting political reform?

In the summer of 1914 the British public was probably less concerned about the rumblings of dissent in Central Europe and more preoccupied with domestic problems such as the unrest in Ireland caused by the Home Rule issue and the infringement of law and order due to the suffrage campaign by the WSPU. The militancy of the suffragettes had hardened since 1912 as government resistance to their demands for the vote persisted. Politicians' reluctance to concede women the vote whilst women attacked public property and caused criminal damage was reflected in the failure of W.H. Dickinson's Representation of the People Bill in 1913, which would have included women's suffrage, to reach the statute books.

War split the suffrage movement. On 7 August 1914, the Home Secretary announced an amnesty for all imprisoned suffragettes on condition that they abided within the law. With the threat of arrest eliminated, Christabel Pankhurst returned from exile in Paris. Very soon, two factions had developed within the suffrage movement – the patriots and the pacifists – over whether they should support military action or not.

a) Patriotism Versus Pacifism: the New Causes

After war was declared, Mrs. Pankhurst surprised both government and her supporters by announcing the cessation of all militant activity. In a rush of patriotism, the Pankhursts embarked on recruitment campaigns urging men to enlist and women to enrol in the munitions factories. Mrs. Pankhurst also became an enthusiastic follower of Lloyd George, liaising with him to encourage more women to work in the munitions industry as well as masterminding the 'Right to Work March' in July 1915 (see page 16). The message of the WSPU was further advertised through its newspaper, which changed its name from *The Suffragette* to *Britannia* in October 1915 and became a vehicle for jingoism and anti-German sentiment. However, not all members of the WSPU agreed with such patriotic fervour. Sylvia Pankhurst, leader of the East London Federation, managed to adhere to her strong pacifist beliefs throughout the war believing that relief work in the East End for working-class women and the destitute was of greater importance.

For the NUWSS, the question of pro- or anti-war attitudes was more divisive. Their leader, Millicent Garrett Fawcett, argued for a patriotic response, believing that it was their duty to support the country in its hour of need. She also anticipated that such loyalty would create the opportunity for women to demonstrate their worthiness for the vote. Yet at a NUWSS Council meeting in November 1914, Fawcett encountered opposition to a proposed motion which defined the war as a battle for 'representative government' and 'progressive democracy', causes which she believed the society should support. Fawcett invoked further dissent when she resisted attempts to send delegates to a convention of the International Women's Suffrage Alliance in The Hague at which calls for peace would be discussed. Members could only attend as individuals not as representatives of the NUWSS.

The pacifists within the movement were a resolute group. Key personalities such as Helena Swanwick, Isabella Ford, Catherine Marshall, and Alice Clark advocated either total opposition to the war or, at the very least, an early negotiated peace. They were disheartened by Mrs. Fawcett's persistent and public endorsement of the war, and her exploitation of her position within the movement to win over support for her views, despite the fact that the pacifists were in the majority. In early March 1915, all the officers of the Union except the President and the Treasurer resigned. Then, at a Special Council meeting in June 1915, Mrs. Fawcett won a motion which committed the NUWSS to war relief work, and rejected any involvement in anti-war activities. Virtually all the remaining pacifists resigned and in late 1915 several of them established the Women's International League for Peace and Freedom headed by Helena Swanwick. The aim of this organisation was to promote peace, internationalism and democratic suffrage on the grounds that war destroyed the principles of democracy.

In her book, *The Cause* (1928), Ray Strachey, a keen supporter of the NUWSS, claimed that the fragmentation of the movement was merely a minor setback. Support for the war amongst the rank and file was supposedly widespread and, in her view, a valuable precondition to securing support for the long-term goal of women's suffrage. Strachey asserted that the patriotic stance of the NUWSS entitled it to represent the 'women's cause' before an increasingly sympathetic government. She assumed therefore that the patriotic approach of the NUWSS was instrumental in gaining them a position of influence once the government began to reconsider electoral reform. But was such an analysis sufficient? Might there not have been far more complex reasons as to why women finally won the vote in 1918?

b) The Political Prize: Women's Suffrage

Both the 'patriots' within the WSPU and the NUWSS tried to claim some credit for the government's eventual enactment of suffrage reform. In their interpretation of events, the NUWSS emphasised the benefits of women's patriotism. According to *The Cause*, anti-suffrage opinion had diminished due to women's willing contributions to the affairs of the nation.

1 From all parts of the country, evidence is constantly reaching our head-
   quarters of Anti-Suffragists dropping their opposition to the full citizenship of women, and assigning as the reason for this the eagerness of
   women of all classes to take their share in the national burden and
5 national sufferings caused by the war, coupled with the professional and
   industrial capacity of women, their adaptability, courage and endurance.
   These things have made a deep impression on the public mind, and have
   done more than anything else to produce the great change in public
   opinion on Women's Suffrage, of which everyone is conscious.[6]

The moderate approach of the NUWSS was also acclaimed as a major factor behind the success in persuading the government to accede to women's suffrage. The combination of Mrs. Fawcett's regular negotiations which she held with the government, plus the resumption of suffrage meetings across the country, was perceived as having a positive effect on government opinion.

The WSPU was likewise prepared to accept compromise. But other factors were said to have played a part in influencing the government. According to Christabel Pankhurst, it was the fear of a resumption of militancy between 1916 and 1918 which was a key reason behind the politicians' decision to grant the vote. The fact that the WSPU had conducted such an effective campaign before 1914 stood as a sharp reminder of what could be revived if the government proved unwilling to grant reform.

But how valid were these interpretations? What were the other developments and changes in attitudes which perhaps created the conditions in which reform at last seemed appropriate? The first question to consider is the extent to which political attitudes were now more in favour of women's suffrage. Pre-war politicians, especially the Liberals, had been wary of enfranchising women in case they voted for the opposition party. But war had produced consensus politics with the creation of coalition government, first in May 1915 under Asquith and then secondly under Lloyd George in December 1916. There was less need to adhere to party politics. Appointments to Cabinet posts also reflected the changing climate; Asquith included Arthur Henderson whilst Lloyd George brought in Bonar Law and Balfour, all three pro-suffragists. Even Asquith, the veteran opponent of female enfranchisement, modified his objections, asserting that women had a 'special claim' to represent their own interests, especially in the coming difficult years of post-war reconstruction. Their assistance in prosecuting the war deserved to be recognised. However, one staunch opponent, Sir F. Banbury, remarked:

1 It has been stated that women require the vote in order to prepare for the change of circumstances which will take place after the War, and that without the vote they will not be able to exercise that influence which they are entitled to exercise on their own behalf. The vote, in my
5 humble opinion ... is not a reward to be given because somebody has done something which is meritorious. It should be given because the people to whom it is given have shown that they are fit and capable to exercise the duty which is thrust upon them – that is to say, that they are fit and capable of using the vote, not in their own personal interests,
10 but in the interests of the country as a whole.[7]

In contrast, Lord Hugh Cecil claimed:

1 If you do not give women suffrage, then in Parliamentary discussions in the future on industrial and other questions, with which great bodies of women are concerned, every Member of Parliament would be subject to the bias, which operates sometimes consciously and sometimes
5 unconsciously on the mind of a Member of Parliament, that if he treats badly the female workers who are not his constituents he will not suffer, while if he treats the men badly ... he will suffer a great deal.[8]

The second point to appreciate is the impact of the war itself on the electoral process. The disruption of war had rendered the electoral registers redundant; thousands of soldiers and sailors were disenfranchised by their inability to comply with the residency requirements for voting. By 1916 the government realised that a complete review of the registers was necessary otherwise at the next general election huge numbers of potential male voters would be unable to exercise their right to vote. Thus practical problems arising from the dislocating effects of war prompted members of the Cabinet to re-examine the conditions for the franchise.

The third issue to consider is the precise role played by the government in introducing female suffrage. Although the political climate was more favourable towards reform, change would not occur unless politicians were willing to act. The first step was to set up a Speaker's Conference in the autumn of 1916 with the remit to examine parliamentary reform. Some of its members were pro-suffragists, and the key question was whether they could persuade the Conference to recommend women's suffrage as well. But although the Conference did finally agree in principle to women's suffrage, they rejected the idea of equal suffrage for men and women. Instead, it was proposed that only women who were household occupiers or wives of occupiers should be enfranchised. Furthermore, the franchise would have to be restricted to women aged 50 and above. At this point, the conservatism of the suffrage movement emerged. Whereas suffragist Sylvia Pankhurst still aspired to full adult equality, other suffrage leaders, in particular Millicent Fawcett, were prepared to compromise, afraid of jeopardising their chances of reform. Her one successful effort, according to Ray Strachey, was to persuade the government to lower the age limit to 30 years.

The final factor which assisted the discussions was the supportive tone within the national press. In contrast to the sometimes vitriolic coverage of the suffrage movement pre-1914, certain newspapers now gave their unequivocal support. The *Observer* was one convert and, most notably, *The Times*, under the control of Lord Northcliffe. Their support has to be viewed within the context of the war in that there was a clear correlation between women's war efforts and the changes in opinion. Women had successfully challenged traditional concepts of their role in society, they had broken down gender barriers and they had proven essential in securing victory for the nation. But the rationale for the vote went deeper than just mere reward for hard work. As *The Times* commented when the vote finally received assent in the House of Lords, they had for some time been urging:

1   that the new case for the woman voter should be thoroughly understood throughout the country. That case rests neither on the triumph of agitation, for agitation has long been stilled, nor in the notion, which every patriotic woman resents, that the vote is a mere reward for good
5   behaviour. It is based wholly on the palpable injustices of withholding such protection as the vote affords from a sex which has for the first time taken its full share in the national effort, and will have sufficient difficulty in any case to maintain the position which it has won.[9]

It was, therefore, the complex interaction of a number of different influences and developments which led to the acceptance of women's suffrage. Under the Representation of the People Act 1918, all men aged 21 and over received the vote whilst women over the age of 30 who were either married to men on the local government register or who were themselves on the local government register were enfranchised. Suffragists viewed it as a great moral victory. But that victory had been determined by more than just the actions of keen activists. Although it would be mistaken to view the First World War as a watershed in terms of long-term change, the short-term progress experienced by women had helped to create a more conducive climate for political reform. In addition, the absence of militant protest by women reduced political opposition and helped to persuade the undecided that women could be trusted with the vote. Above all, though, there was an abiding sense that political reform could no longer proceed on the basis of excluding half the population. It was time to include women in the democratic process.

Yet, it must be noted that the politicians had acted with caution. To the frustration of the East London Federation, young and single women received no reward for their sacrifices. The government imposed limitations on the vote in order to ensure that women did not form the majority of the electorate. Likewise, they regarded married women as the essential backbone to future government social policy, in other words the partnership between the wife and the mother in the home. Progress was tempered with conservatism.

4 Social Change

> **KEY ISSUES** To what extent did the war have a liberating influence on women's lives? How did society react to the new responsibilities exercised by women? Did women's lives benefit from the social changes brought about by war, or were the benefits in many respects just superficial?

The wartime experiences of British women can be interpreted as having combined radical change in conjunction with the sustaining of traditional attitudes. In many respects, the realities of everyday life for women between 1914 and 1918 led to greater economic independence. Another consequence of war was the fact that opportunities existed to defy social norms. Social conventions and sexual stereotyping were directly challenged by the exigencies of war.

a) The Advantages of War: New Social Freedoms

Life in wartime Britain brought inevitable hardships. Although women had, before the war, undertaken demanding roles, often providing the vital extra income to sustain their families, they now faced an unprecedented situation. As we have seen, thousands of women were engaged in employment which tested their physical as well as mental strength. In addition, the absence of men at home and work created an environment in which women were compelled to assume responsibilities which were previously the prerogative of men. Women now acted as head of household as well as managing the customary domestic affairs of the family. Wartime shortages complicated people's daily lives, forcing women to juggle the demands of work with the necessity of queuing for food and fuel, arranging child care, the weekly washing, ironing and cleaning. The challenge of coping was in many respects exhausting. Nevertheless, these responsibilities enabled women to assume a new status within society, one which offered greater independence and freedom.

Employment was one of the key facilitators of social change. Improved earnings raised the status of women, granting them a new level of spending power not only for essentials such as food, but also for clothes and entertainment. With independent money, women no longer relied on weekly handouts from their husbands. This inevitably gave women greater self-confidence.

Work also changed women's social environment. Many working-class girls left home for the first time, to be accommodated in hostels or lodgings. Some, such as those at the Woolwich Arsenal, were housed in purpose built estates – the Well Hall estate – whereas others were expected to travel long distances after a long working day. But the whole ethos of living and working in industry added a new dimension to women's lives. The camaraderie of the work's canteen, the social contact within the hostels, the opportunity to enjoy dances and clubs – these gave women a much broader social experience compared with normal home life. Young, single woman especially felt liberated by the absence of chaperones. For middle-class women, volunteer work offered women their first opportunity to break away from home, to travel and to socialise without parental supervision. As Vera Brittain noted in her autobiography, *Testament of Youth*, at the start of the war she and her boyfriend deliberately deceived her parents in order to travel by rail alone between Leicester and Oxford, whereas by the middle of 1915, 'No one suggested going with me to London; already the free and easy movements of girl war-workers had begun to modify convention'.[10]

Jazz clubs flourished and became the venue for the new dance crazes. Smoking and drinking amongst unescorted young women became a familiar sight, although the older generation looked on with disapproval at what seemed frivolous and unseemly behaviour. As one young girl of eighteen commented:

i The theatres at this period produced little but the lightest plays and revues, and many protests were made by the more seriously minded regarding the suggestiveness and impropriety of certain stage productions and the scanty clothing worn by the girls employed. The desire to
5 gamble became stronger and card-playing of all kinds more popular, the games generally chosen being bridge and poker.[11]

Sexual independence was another consequence of less stringent codes of behaviour. Conservative-minded members of society were alarmed by what they perceived to be an increase in immoral behaviour amongst young women. Critics alleged that there had been a rise in the number of illegitimate births, but in reality there was little change compared with pre-war figures. For many women, the absence of the man in the household was welcome. These women not only gained greater self-esteem but respite from domestic strife.

One outcome of the war years was the government's decision to enact social legislation to protect women's welfare. Married women were a crucial element within the workforce, but their labour would be wasted unless better provisions were made for childcare. Some 108 day nurseries, funded up to 75 per cent by the government, were established at munitions factories, whilst infant welfare centres were created by local authorities. These provisions were not motivated by enlightened government beliefs in the intrinsic need to cater for the less fortunate and more vulnerable in the community although they did reflect a continuation of welfare policies commenced during the pre-war era. The fact that these nurseries were largely closed down at the end of the war signified that their main purpose was to facilitate the opportunities for married women to contribute to the war effort. The only long-lasting initiative taken by the government was to pass the Maternity and Child Welfare Act in 1918 which established homes where women could give birth and recuperate, and provided hospital treatment and nurseries for the first time.

b) The Disadvantages of War: the Social Restraints

Women clearly profited during the war from the relaxation of traditional rules of behaviour. In many respects they were able to socialise more independently without jeopardising their reputations. But how far were these changes tolerated as merely a short-term reality of war? Is there any evidence, for example, underlying the praise heaped upon women during the war, that society still viewed women as unreliable citizens for whom the moral guidance of their superiors was necessary?

Women may have welcomed the chance to socialise with men on a more equal footing but approval was not universal. Traditionalists were alarmed by the thought that women would neglect their duties as wives and mothers. Consequently, despite all the propaganda urging women to act for their country in its hour of need, the government also sought to glorify motherhood, emphasising that it was their duty to bear children. Theories about the importance of the purity of race were widely circulating in the early years of the twentieth century and these certainly gave foundation to government concerns that the future success of the nation was dependent upon the production of healthy children.

Such policies were designed primarily for working-class women. In tandem with the increased provision of nursery care for working mothers was the assumption that both their physical and moral health must be protected in order to promote efficient workers and healthy mothers. Whilst increased health care in factories was a positive development – first aid centres enabled many working-class women to access health care on a regular basis – the moral supervision of these women could be interpreted as demeaning and patronising. Within the factories the role of women supervisors, who checked up on absenteeism and lateness amongst employees, was particularly resented.

Supervision went beyond the walls of the workplace. One of the wartime volunteer organisations was the Women's Police Patrols, which undertook to act as moral guardians of women in public.

These patrols exercised extraordinary authority over women's private lives, cautioning women in public places like pubs and parks if they were thought to be behaving in 'an unseemly manner'. Fears that women would get drunk on the separation allowance issued to wives of sailors and soldiers even resulted in curfews being imposed, banning women in some areas from pubs at night or even out on the streets. The existence of this supervision typified the underlying assumptions about young working-class women, namely that unless they were closely watched, such women would indulge in excessive drinking, and licentious behaviour with members of the armed forces. The implication that it was women, rather than men, who were the likely transgressors of acceptable behaviour, indicates that attitudes amongst some people at least had changed very little.

Although the government endeavoured to present a rather glossy image of women's lives during the First World War, creating an impression of willing sacrifice for the sake of the nation, the realities were less glamorous. The strains of managing daily domestic chores with the arduous nature of work meant that life was often a struggle, one which many women were ready to relinquish once the war was over. Whilst for some, an enhanced status within society was a welcome development, for others, there seemed little advantage to such responsibilities.

5 Conclusion

```
KEY ISSUE  How far was the First World War a watershed in
women's lives?
```

The First World War produced a unique environment for women within which many preconceived ideas about the role of women were challenged. Undoubtedly one of the most important changes was the way women now thought about themselves. Although they had gained neither political nor economic equality with men, they had nevertheless demonstrated both to themselves and others that as a sex they were not necessarily inferior. This gave many women vital confidence and self-assurance to seek further reforms in the post-war era. To what did they owe this confidence? In the workplace, women had broken down many barriers, refuting the argument that women were too inept or physically weak to be employed within heavy industry. They had proven themselves indispensable to the war effort. Despite fears to the contrary, the assumption of greater social responsibilities by women did not provoke a degeneration of public and private morals. Instead, women acquired more self-respect; their sense of inferiority diminished. Finally, the long-awaited political goal of women's suffrage was attained in an atmosphere of consensus, with women now regarded, by some at least, as essential contributors to political life. With eight million women now enfranchised, there was an abiding sense that women could at last use their vote to press for essential reforms.

In the short-term, therefore, it could be argued that the war had instigated significant changes in women's lives. Undoubtedly attitudes towards women were jolted out of their nineteenth-century time warp. On one level, the practicalities of war prompted both men and women to readjust their normal expectations as to what status women held in society. But it is questionable whether the war consolidated and secured those developments. In many respects the underlying beliefs of both government and employers had not altered. Their priorities in 1918 were primarily concerned with guaranteeing jobs for the demobilised troops in 1918. In order to effect that policy, women would have to return to their domestic roles. Even with the granting of the franchise, the underlying beliefs of the government were clear. Political equality with men would have created an electoral female majority within the country. Most politicians could not envisage that entrusting all women with the vote would safeguard parliamentary government. Thus women's political contributions to the life of the nation were carefully proscribed by the limits of the 1918 legislation. Ultimately, though, the extent of women's progress would only become apparent after the country had returned to peacetime conditions. It is those conditions and experiences which will be evaluated in Chapters 3 and 4.

References

1 Monica Cosens, *Lloyd George's Munition Girls* (Hutchinson, 1916), p. 8.
2 Gail Braybon, *Women Workers in the First World War* (Croom Helm, 1981), p. 46.
3 Gilbert Stone, ed, *Women War Workers* (Harrap, 1917), p. 44.
4 *The Common Cause*, 24 March 1916, vol VII, p. 658.
5 Quoted in L.K. Yates, *The Woman's Part* (Hodder & Stoughton, 1918), p. 35.
6 *The Common Cause*, 19 May 1916, vol VIII, no.371, p. 82.
7 *Hansard's Parliamentary Debates*, 5th Series, vol. XCIV, 19 June 1917, col. 164.
8 *Ibid.*, col. 1662.
9 *The Times*, 10 January 1918, p. 7.
10 Vera Brittain, *Testament of Youth* (Fontana, 1980), p. 177.
11 Mrs. C.S. Peel, *How We Lived Then 1914–1918* (John Lane, The Bodley Head Ltd., 1929), pp. 70–71.

Summary Diagram
The First World War, 1914–18

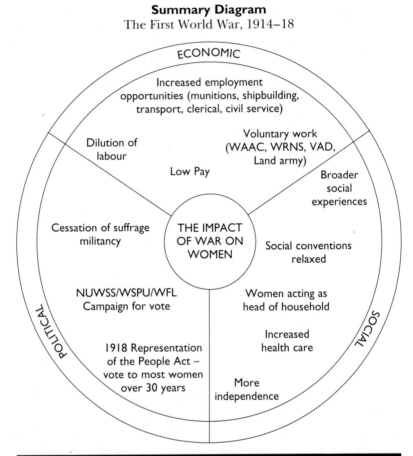

ECONOMIC

Increased employment
opportunities (munitions, shipbuilding,
transport, clerical, civil service)

Dilution of
labour

Voluntary work
(WAAC, WRNS, VAD,
Land army)

Low Pay

Broader
social
experiences

Cessation of suffrage
militancy

THE IMPACT
OF WAR ON
WOMEN

Social conventions
relaxed

NUWSS/WSPU/WFL
Campaign for vote

Women acting as
head of household

POLITICAL

1918 Representation
of the People Act –
vote to most women
over 30 years

Increased
health care

More
independence

SOCIAL

Working on Chapter 2

You now need to work more closely on each of the three main sections in this chapter, taking each one as a key heading. First, ensure that you have a sound factual grasp of key information. Use the sub-headings as a guide and identify the relevant information with bullet points. You should concentrate on the following: the main economic and social changes affecting women; the policies and ideas of the suffrage movements; important government decisions regarding franchise reform.

Next, you need to evaluate the central themes of the chapter: i) how far did the war transform women's lives? ii) was the war merely an instigator of short-term rather than long-term change? iii) how far did attitudes of both men and women regarding women's role in society change as a result of the war? As indicated in the key issues, this requires you to think about underlying influences as well as the pragmatic responses to the necessities of war and to understand the effect each had on the other. Within each category, economic, political and social, try and establish the *extent* of change affecting women, whether the motives for change reflected significant shifts in attitudes, and whether progress was merely a response to the effects of war or the result of more fundamental influences.

Source-based questions on Chapter 2

1. Employment of Women
Read the extracts by Monica Cosens on pages 17 and the NUWSS extract on page 21 and examine the illustration on page 19. Answer the following questions.

a) With reference to the illustration on page 19, explain briefly what this reveals about the 'dilution' of labour during the First World War. (*3 marks*)
b) Why, according to Monica Cosens, was 'handling a machine' in line 6 such a challenge? (*3 marks*)
c) How useful is the extract on page 21 as an example of women's ability to do 'men's' work? (5 marks)
d) Using all three sources and your own knowledge, assess the extent to which both female and male attitudes towards women's employment were altered by the impact of war. (*9 marks*)

Hints and advice: The first two questions should be quite straightforward. They test recall and historical understanding of women's employment during the First World War. Check the marks for each question and ensure that you include sufficient points to earn those marks. The last two questions require you to evaluate the utility of sources and to test their reliability by deploying your own knowledge. With Question 1c, you need to appreciate who wrote the source; you should consider carefully why the source was written. In Question 1d) the three sources are intended to stimulate further discussion regarding attitudes towards women's work. For example the patriotism of Monica Cosens is very clear, but you would need to analyse whether or not this was a typical response of women working during the war. At face value, the illustration may not seem to reveal a great deal, but the source should be used as a tool with which to develop further discussion.

2. The Franchise
Read the extracts by Sir F. Banbury and Lord Hugh Cecil and *The Times* on pages 25–6.

a) What does Banbury mean when he refers to 'something which is meritorious' (line 6)? (*3 marks*)
b) Explain what is meant by 'the triumph of agitation' in the extract from *The Times* (lines 2–3). (*3 marks*)
c) In your opinion, which of these three sources support the view that democracy in Britain was deficient? (*6 marks*)
d) Using these sources and your own knowledge, judge how reliable these sources are in explaining why some women got the vote in 1918. (*8 marks*)

3 Political Advances in the Inter-War Years

POINTS TO CONSIDER

This chapter examines the effect of the franchise on women during the 1920s and 1930s with respect to their involvement in both national and local politics. In order to judge women's success in becoming active citizens you will need to understand first the part played by women themselves in gaining access to the political scene, and second the responses of governments and political parties to female enfranchisement. As you read the chapter, see if you can construct a checklist which sets out the political gains and setbacks incurred by women during this period.

KEY DATES

1918	**Feb**	Representation of the People Act.
	21 Nov	Parliament (Qualification of Women) Act.
	14 Dec	General Election – only one woman elected.
1919	**Oct**	Election of Nancy Astor, first woman MP.
1923	**Dec**	5 women elected to Parliament.
1924	**Jan**	First Labour government.
		Margaret Bondfield became Parliamentary Secretary in the Ministry of Labour.
	Oct	Conservative government – Katharine Atholl became Parliamentary Secretary at the Board of Education.
1926	**July**	Equal Rights Procession in Hyde Park.
1928		Representation of the People (Equal Franchise) Act.
1929		Local Government Act.
1931		15 women elected to Parliament.
1935	**Nov**	Last General Election before the Second World War – 9 women MPs elected.

1 Introduction

The passing of the Representation of the People Act in February 1918 marked the successful culmination of a long and consistent campaign to achieve women's franchise. However, the initial euphoria surrounding the acquisition of the vote soon wore off as women confronted the realities of national and local politics. New challenges emerged during the inter-war years which impeded women's hopes of gaining political equality with men.

The most immediate issue facing the women's movement was the need to ensure that women were encouraged to use their vote. The next stage was to overcome predictable resistance to the election of women MPs. This necessitated a change of attitude within political parties towards the adoption of women as prospective candidates as well as encouraging women themselves to seek a political career. Even when women were elected, there was the question of whether women could play an effective role within Parliament, particularly when they were in a minority. Another objective was the task of persuading politicians to end the franchise discrimination against women under 30, especially as men had the vote at 21. Despite numerous difficulties, this campaign was eventually successful. Yet equal franchise did not necessarily bring the anticipated results. Although the main political parties recognised the importance of wooing the female vote, both the Conservatives and Labour were very skilful in marginalising women and gaining their acquiescence in what continued to be male-directed policies. As a result, women's main contribution, both in national and local politics, was primarily, although not exclusively, in the areas of social and economic issues. It is women's responses to the above challenges and the reasons for their successes and failures which will be evaluated during the course of this chapter.

2 The 1918 General Election

> **KEY ISSUES** How were women encouraged to vote in 1918 and why was it so difficult to get women elected to Parliament?

a) Mobilising the Women's Vote

On 14 November 1918, three days after the Armistice, the government announced that it would hold the first general election in eight years on 14 December. For 8.5 million women, this decision provided the first chance to exercise a direct political influence rather than an implied influence through the votes of their male family members. Political involvement was further facilitated by the successful enactment of the Parliament (Qualification of Women) Act, which passed on 21 November 1918, enabling women over the age of 21 to stand as parliamentary candidates. This created the strange situation that a woman could become an MP before she was eligible to vote.

A daunting task lay ahead. Since candidates had to be nominated by 4 December, the organisational timetable was extremely tight. Experienced political parties possessed the necessary party machinery to implement effective parliamentary campaigns at short notice. For women, this was all unproven territory.

Suffrage organisations recognised the urgent need for political education. Apart from the NUWSS, other organisations such as the London Society for Women's Suffrage and Women's Citizens' Associations (WCA), founded in 1917, embarked on a programme of publicising women's rights, detailing the process of vote registration and raising awareness of the political issues which women should now address. The need for active participation was stressed in order that women could fully exploit their new entitlement.

The suffrage societies were resolved that the prejudice of male politicians should not deter the inexperienced female voter. Women were encouraged to make independent judgements and critical appraisals of parliamentary candidates' commitments to rectifying inequalities affecting women. Lists of questions were issued with which women could challenge and seek clarification of candidates' policies. The Women's Freedom League (WFL), through its paper *The Vote*, claimed that:

1 In most constituencies women are attending the meetings of all candidates impartially, and are questioning them on matters of special interest to women, and of national, not personal importance ... Where there are no women candidates, women voters are already making
5 their influence felt, and we urge them to continue to question men candidates and secure their public pledges that if returned to the House of Commons they will work for the removal of all women's political, civil, and professional disabilities ... [1]

The emphasis on obtaining pledges from parliamentary candidates had been a cornerstone of suffrage policy prior to 1918. It continued to underlie their approach thereafter, signifying a continued faith in the concept of democratic change through the parliamentary process.

b) The Women Candidates

There were just over three weeks in which to prepare for the election. 17 women stood as candidates. Emmeline Pethick-Lawrence represented Labour, as did Charlotte Despard, the President of the WFL, and Mary Macarthur, a leading trade unionist. Emily Phipps, President of the National Federation of Women Teachers, and Ray Strachey were two of the six Independent candidates, reflecting the historic trend within the women's movement to adhere to non-party lines. Christabel Pankhurst, as a candidate for the Women's Party, was the only person to receive the 'coupon' – official approval from the Coalition government. Women's groups supported these candidates enthusiastically, holding public meetings, and distributing pamphlets and questionnaires, but overcoming endemic hostility and prejudice was problematic. Despite their considerable expertise either as activists within the suffrage movement or as leaders within independent organisations, none of these women could hope to compete on equal terms with seasoned parliamentary male campaigners. With one exception they were all defeated, although Mary Macarthur only lost by 1,333 votes.

The one success was barely a cause for celebration. The victor, Countess Constance Markievicz, who was an active supporter of Sinn

Fein, had conducted her campaign from the confines of Holloway prison and, once elected, announced in accordance with the policy of all other elected Sinn Feiners that she would not take up her seat at Westminster as this would entail recognition of the British crown and its right to rule Ireland.

c) Implications for the Future

Amongst women's groups, the post-mortem on the election produced few surprises. They suffered from a lack of extensive party machinery, essential for any successful campaign, from inadequate funds, and inexperience at fighting elections. In addition, they had discovered the handicap of fighting in unwinnable seats, a consequence of the main parties' reluctance to risk allocating a safe seat to a woman. It was also unclear whether candidates should be affiliated to one of the main political parties or operate independently as a women's party. The former option posed the risk that party political issues would predominate over those concerning women. Yet if women pursued the non-party approach, would not continued discrimination and distrust of women as politicians act against them? The experiences of the 1918 campaign did at least serve one very useful purpose. It demonstrated all too clearly that the objective of empowering women was still a distant goal.

3 Women in Parliament

> **KEY ISSUES** Who were the women elected to Parliament in the inter-war years and why were they elected? How effective were they as politicians?

a) The First Female Members of Parliament

The disappointment surrounding the failure of several leading feminists to win a seat in the House of Commons was further compounded by the fact that the first woman to take a seat in Parliament had no connections with the suffrage movement. Indeed, she was not even born in Britain. Nancy Astor, an American, was married to Waldorf Astor who, on the death of his father in October 1919, inherited a seat in the House of Lords and so had to resign his parliamentary seat for the Sutton Division of Plymouth. When Nancy Astor agreed to replace her husband in the ensuing by-election, she immediately faced criticism that a married woman with children should not enter the House of Commons. Her robust retort was indicative of the combative style which she adopted during debates after her election:

ı I have heard it said that a woman who has got children shouldn't go into
the House of Commons. She ought to be at home looking after her children. That is true, but I feel someone ought to be looking after the more
unfortunate children. My children are among the fortunate ones, and it
5 is that that steels me to go to the House of Commons to fight the fight,
not only of the men but of the women and children of England![2]

In analysing the circumstances in which Nancy Astor was successfully
elected, certain key points emerge. The first consideration is her
motives for seeking election. She did not hold any strong convictions
about the importance of getting women into Parliament. She stood as
her husband's wife, intending to perpetuate continuity of representation within his constituency. Second, she was chosen because of the
status she held within a well-known family, not because she had
proven her standing as an independent person.

This link with the family was equally applicable to the women who
entered parliament between 1921 and 1923. When the Liberal MP for
Louth died in 1921, his widow, Mrs. Wintringham, retained his seat in
the subsequent by-election. Likewise, in 1923 the Liberal MP for
Berwick-upon-Tweed was compelled to relinquish his seat, only to be
swiftly followed by his wife, Mrs. Mabel Hilton Philipson, who stood as
a Conservative and won. What, therefore, can we conclude about
these trends? Essentially, it was very difficult for women around 1919
to gain respect in politics unless they came from a background of
family power and influence, and had the advantage of a sympathy
vote within a supportive constituency. For women to act independently without the back-up of the local party machinery was still too
ambitious. It was, as yet, too early for women to enter the public world
purely through their own personal achievements.

b) A New Cohort of MPs

As with all political reforms, there was a predictable time lag between
the enactment of legislation and its eventual impact on practical politics. Between 1918 and 1922 only a handful of women entered parliament. Indeed, at the general election of 1922, the number of women
MPs did not change at all. But there was a discernible shift regarding
both the backgrounds of female candidates and their motives for seeking election, most notably amongst those elected in December 1923.

The most remarkable difference was that, unlike their predeces-
sors, these women sought election to parliament as individuals in
their own right rather than as surrogate males. Three out of the five
women elected were members of the Labour Party, each with a background of either Labour activism or suffrage agitation. Margaret
Bondfield, a trade unionist, had been the only woman delegate to the
TUC in 1899 before subsequently joining and working for Mary
Macarthur's National Federation of Women Workers. Susan

Lawrence was the first woman elected to the London County Council in 1910, although she then abandoned her allegiance to the Conservative Party and moved to Labour because of 'Conservative indifference to low wages and bad conditions of women cleaners in the London schools'.[3] Dorothy Jewson, a graduate of Girton College, was a keen feminist. Of the two remaining MPs, one was Lady Vera Terrington, who had conducted an effective campaign for the Liberals. She had attacked the cornerstone of Prime Minister Baldwin's election manifesto – protective taxes, or tariff reform, on imported food: 'under tariff reform the housewife would not know from one week to another what things would cost'.[4] Finally, Katharine, Duchess of Atholl, won the West Perthshire constituency for the Conservative Party by 150 votes, having previously gained valuable experience on local government committees.

Overall, the number of women elected to parliament during the inter-war years remained depressingly low. Although eight women were elected in December 1923, this number was halved in October 1924. Women's greatest success was in 1931 when 15 (2.4 per cent of all MPs) were returned to parliament (see illustration on page 40). In 1935, the number was reduced to nine; a further four gained seats in by-elections between 1935 and 1938. Unfortunately little was done by the main political parties to facilitate women's careers in politics. Of the main political parties, Labour gave women the most positive support but even the policies of socialism conflicted with the aspirations of feminism (see pages 63–70).

c) Women's Careers in Parliament

Historians generally agree that women MPs focused predominantly on securing family and welfare legislation. Most women's direct experience of tackling inequality was in the area of domestic social and economic problems – divorce, child care, education and public health. Women's authority on such issues had long been recognised in local government. Now it was transferred to national politics.

The wealth of legislation passed during the 1920s which targeted these concerns was impressive. Nancy Astor, for example, was no ardent feminist, yet once elected she argued for a range of benefits to improve the lives of women and children. She actively campaigned on questions of personal morality such as prostitution and temperance, as well as encouraging nursery education and improvements in housing and public health. One of her most positive legislative contributions was on temperance. In 1923 she managed, with the help of her husband in the House of Lords, to oversee the Intoxicating Liquor (Sale to Persons under Eighteen) Bill through parliament which, with just one amendment, imposed more stringent age restrictions on the sale of alcohol to young persons. Although 16 to 18 year olds could still purchase beer or cider in a public house, with the exception of

Victorious MPs in 1931

the bar, in all other respects this legislation resembled the laws which still apply today.

Margaret Bondfield was the first woman appointed to a government post when she became Parliamentary Secretary at the Ministry of Labour in the 1924 Labour government. She was subsequently Minister of Labour in the second Labour government, 1929. But as members of the Labour Party, both she and her contemporaries were primarily concerned with resolving general problems such as that of unemployment, rather than the specific problems encountered by unemployed women. In 1931, for example, Bondfield was criticised because she supported MacDonald and the Chancellor, Philip Snowden, by voting for a bill which would deprive some married women of unemployment benefits. Her record as a Labour minister was not impressive and so, like many Labour MPs who lost the confidence of the electorate during the National Government crisis of 1931, she was defeated at the subsequent election.

During her career, Ellen Wilkinson acquired a commendable record for pursuing the rights of both men and women. She made important contributions to the Widows, Orphans and Old Age Contributory Pensions Bill in 1925 and, like Nancy Astor, sought to get more women police appointed. Wilkinson shocked the Commons during the Second Reading of the Coal Mines (Hours) Bill when she displayed the 'guss', the coil of rope, chain and hook which miners had to wear round their legs in order to haul carts of coal. She likewise made an impassioned plea on behalf of her Jarrow constituents after she had accompanied them in 1936 on the famous Jarrow March to Westminster in protest over unemployment.

Another successful parliamentarian was the Duchess of Atholl. When Stanley Baldwin formed a Conservative government in October 1924, he surprised politicians by selecting Katharine Atholl to be Parliamentary Secretary of State at the Board of Education, so ignoring the more experienced Nancy Astor. She went on to make many positive interventions regarding educational funding, defending her department against impending government cuts.

Although other renowned women also made their mark in politics – Edith Summerskill, Ruth Dalton, Jennie Lee and Eleanor Rathbone to name but a few – it would be impossible to evaluate the careers of all the women who sat in the Commons between 1919 and 1939. However, despite the poor state of female representation, their achievements merit recognition. Women continued to face enormous obstacles to securing a political career and, once in Parliament, had to contend with the ever-familiar problems of male prejudice and reluctance to treat women as equals (see pages 42–3). The Commons remained a bastion of male influence where few concessions were made by an overwhelmingly male establishment to the presence of women. Essentially, women had to behave as 'honorary men', adjusting to the long working hours and coping with the intimidating comments they often received. They were also excluded from informal consultations, as the MP, Thelma Cazalet-Keir discovered.

1 When I entered the House there was still something freakish about a woman M.P., and I frequently saw male colleagues pointing me out to their friends as though I were a sort of giant panda ... Not one of the dozen or so women M.Ps ever entered the Smoking Room where, so
5 rumour had it, as much constructive business is transacted as on the floor of the House.[5]

For a woman to be successful in politics, she had to possess a sense of mission, whether it was socialism, feminism or just personal political ambition and perseverance. As Edith Summerskill noted after her election, 'Parliament, with its conventions and protocol, seemed a little like a boys' school which had decided to take a few girls. Woe betide the new-comer who forgot the rules'.[6]

4 The Campaign for Equal Franchise

> **KEY ISSUES** What arguments and tactics did women's organisations deploy prior to 1928 in their campaign for equal franchise? Why did it take so long to secure this reform?

Feminists had been left in no doubt that their modest achievements in 1918 would be of little long-term significance unless they could sustain the current momentum of support and gain full citizenship for women. Two major deficiencies in the 1918 Act had to be addressed. First, the age requirement excluded the young, single women who had worked in industry and whose efforts had been so applauded by politicians at the end of the war. Second, the stipulation that women aged 30 and over had to be either local government electors or married to such an elector meant that many professional single women living in rented accommodation were voteless. When equal suffrage was finally granted in 1928, an extra 1.95 million women over the age of 30 were added to the electoral register.

a) Lobbying for Equality

The first attempt to redress the inequalities of the 1918 Act occurred in 1919 when Labour introduced the Women's Emancipation Bill, permitting women aged 21 and over to vote. Despite a Commons majority of 12, it failed to reach the statute books. A second chance emerged in February 1920, with a proposed amendment to the Representation of the People Bill again lowering the voting age of women to twenty-one. The themes of the debate had a familiar tone: that women were equal in intelligence and ability to men; that women could now demonstrate equal standing with men in term of careers such as medicine, science, languages and arts. As one supporter asserted, there were many blatant inconsistencies in the 1918 Act:

1 The effect of the restriction of the women's parliamentary vote to the age of thirty was to keep off the register the great mass of industrial working women. It was claimed that the vote was given to women by the 1918 Act as a recognition of their industrial service during the War.
5 I should place the recognition of women to vote on an equality with men on a much higher plane than industrial work during the War. As an actual fact, only about one in fifteen of the industrial working women were enfranchised. The great mass of the factory and office workers among women are under thirty years of age, and many of those over
10 thirty have not the necessary local government qualifications under the 1918 Act. It is estimated that 90 per cent of the women now on the register are wives in the homes of the country, and that single women are still largely disfranchised. The retention of the occupational qualification for local government affects the women adversely, as their
15 Parliamentary vote depends on their husband's local government qualification.[7]

Rectifying these anomalies was one justification for reform. The belief that women had already demonstrated their responsibilities as mature citizens was another. Yet on-going prejudice still prevailed, in particular the assertion that younger women were too irrational to vote. One male MP claimed: 'Girls of twenty-one are ... far more emotional than men of the same age'.[8] Moreover, there was the argument that equal enfranchisement would place women in a majority thereby placing an unacceptable distribution of power in their favour. In contrast, however, the current majority enjoyed by men was not contentious. One MP speculated that a female majority could result in such a disastrous policy as prohibition, when all alcohol was banned in the United States.

As with so many other amendments debated by the Commons on this topic prior to 1914, its chances of success were totally dependent on the goodwill of the current government which, once again, was not forthcoming. The Annual Report of the National Union of Societies for Equal Citizenship (formerly the NUWSS) was swift to condemn the government for breaking its election pledges to 'remove all existing inequalities in the law as between men and women'.[9]

Bitter disappointment reinforced the determination of the suffrage organisations first to persist with their programme of political education for women so that women would agitate for the vote and second to sustain a well co-ordinated campaign of petitions, demonstrations and protests to Parliament. The NUSEC's parliamentary secretary, Mrs. Eva Hubback, was very active in encouraging deputations to Parliament, reporting back to her members on the progress of bills, and sending circulars and letters to MPs.

In January 1924 hopes were raised when Labour formed a minority government. Shortly thereafter a Private Member's Bill proposing equal suffrage won second place in the Private Members' ballot to be debated in the Commons. To the intense disappointment of the suffrage groups, the bill fell victim to government apathy and was eventually lost due to delays in the Committee stage of the bill, the onset of the summer recess and the collapse of the Labour government in October 1924. As analysts of that first Labour tenure of power have concluded, Labour was so anxious to demonstrate its capabilities as a party of government that it refrained from alienating opinion. Women's equal suffrage was not deemed to be a decisive vote-winner.

There were some grounds for optimism. During the election campaign, Stanley Baldwin issued a press statement which stated Conservative Party support for franchise reform. But the omission from the King's Speech, as the new Parliament convened in November 1924, of any proposal to summon a conference on constitutional reform served yet again as a reminder of the fickle nature of politics.

In 1925 the NUSEC applied further pressure on the government. They published a pamphlet entitled *The Case for Equal Franchise* which highlighted the disabilities affecting so many women, in particular, those women who still worked in industry:

Every year Parliament is considering matters such as the Factory Bill, the Lead Paint Bill, and the administration of Unemployment Insurance, which immediately affect the conditions under which our industrial women work. In some cases the interests of women workers clash with

5 those of men workers, but as long as every Member of Parliament
knows that he has many more men wage-earners in his constituency,
how can he be expected to take as much care to interpret the wishes
of his women constituents as those of his male constituents? [10]

Such problems could only be rectified by granting equal political
rights.

Suffragists were particularly worried that the Conservatives were
opposed to granting the 'flapper' vote (to apparently irresponsible
young single women under 30), as this would undermine political
stability. When a compromise age restriction of 25 and over for
women was suggested, the propaganda activity of all the suffrage
organisations intensified against the idea. A concerted campaign co-
ordinated by the NUSEC and involving a network of affiliated societies such as the WCA, the WFL and the Six Point Group (SPG) was
launched, with a major gathering at Central Hall Westminster in
February 1926. During the coming months, they canvassed politicians' support, extracting pledges from potential sympathisers, and
targeting those who were as yet unconvinced. The Women' Freedom
League held regular Sunday morning meetings in Hyde Park and on
3 July 1926 a large-scale Equal Rights Procession and Demonstration
took place in Hyde Park attended by 3,500 women. In her analysis of
this suffrage meeting, Cheryl Law observed:

1 The procession was a reminder of the underlying unity of the extraordinary network which the women's movement had created in less than
60 years. The differences of party and non-party, industrial working
class and professional middle class; welfare and equalitarian; militant and
5 constitutionalist were reconciled, or at least laid to one side. [11]

Intense propaganda activity was sustained in the ensuing months and
in March 1927 Baldwin agreed to receive a deputation of women after
which he promised to place an equal franchise bill before the
Commons. He also agreed with pragmatists within his party that it
would be politically disastrous to persist with the 25 year old limit. If
women were to become the electoral majority, then it might be tacti-
cally advantageous if an age limit of 21 was conceded under a
Conservative rather than a Labour government.

Nevertheless, the suffrage organisations could see that securing the
bill would not be straightforward as there were sharp divisions within
the government. Opposition from the conservative press, especially
the *Daily Mail*, which did its best to depict the younger women as emotional individuals whose ill-considered decisions would wreck sound
government, also had to be countered. Their lobbying was maintained up to the last minute with deputations to Parliament, plus
demonstrations in Whitehall and a petition to Baldwin on the day the
bill was introduced. in March 1928. The Representation of the People
(Equal Franchise) Act was finally secured on 2 July 1928. Not even

die-hard Conservatives could prevent women from attaining their long-awaited right to full citizenship.

b) An Assessment of the Suffrage Campaign

Opinions differ regarding the extent to which the women's suffrage campaign was responsible for securing the 1928 Act. As will be seen in Section 5, the political parties had invested interests in trying to attract the women's vote. Political expediency, therefore, has to be regarded as a major factor in persuading both Labour and Conservatives to cease their ambiguity towards reform and to give equal franchise their eventual assent. Another viewpoint is that the implicit majority in favour of equal franchise, which had prevailed for decades, was translated into an actual majority primarily because opposition seemed less tenable in an age when women were finally improving their standing in society.

Yet how significant was the organised pressure from the suffrage societies? According to Cheryl Law and other feminist historians, there was a considerable degree of continuity within the suffrage movement from pre-war to post-war campaigns. Although activism was less militant after 1918, suffrage societies had maintained a co-ordinated and law-abiding campaign with pressure applied regularly on politicians.

5 Women and the Political Parties

> **KEY ISSUES** Why did no Women's Party emerge within Parliament? How did the main political parties react to women voters and politicians?

The political advances of women during the inter-war years depended not only on their success in becoming active citizens, but also on the parties' response to this new dimension in British politics. Voting power and a few female MPs alone would not be sufficient to alter male political thinking. The crucial question was whether male politicians would now give women positive assistance so that they could claim their share of responsibility within the parties.

a) The Failure to Establish a Women's Party

Amongst the first group of women candidates in the 1918 election, a fair number (six out of 17) had stood as Independents, rather than being affiliated to one of the main political parties. With so many women's organisations in existence, there was a definite anticipation that a cross-party women's group, transcending party politics and pursuing specific women's interests, would develop.

This expectation did not materialise as women MPs were rapidly subsumed into the intricacies of party politics. Party loyalty, especially within the Labour Party, was considered to be of higher priority than the interests of one faction. Such demands presented many women MPs with an unwelcome dilemma. The danger would be that without active promotion of women's issues, these important questions would remain in the background. Yet if they neglected the overall party's interests or indeed the concerns of their male constituents, it would not be a good personal recommendation when they stood for re-selection. Ultimately, therefore, women's political futures rested within the mainstream parties. What mattered was the reception accorded to women by Labour and the Conservatives.

b) The Labour Party

Prior to 1918, Labour women had hoped that they could co-ordinate an independent approach to women's interests within the Labour Party. But in 1918 Labour published a new constitution which ensured that women were just one of many affiliated groups to the party. Women's Sections were established from which four women were permitted to sit on the National Executive – the policy making body within the party – although they were outnumbered by the trade unions, socialist societies and local labour parties. Hannah Mitchell, later a well-respected local councillor in Manchester, wrote indignantly in her autobiography, *The Hard Way Up* (1968), that she was not prepared to sacrifice women's political independence for the purpose of party unity and so joined the Independent Labour Party, which was more open to both sexes.

Feminists within the Labour Party faced a huge dilemma. The party's main objective was to address inequalities and discriminatory legislation through its policies of collectivism and socialism. As committed socialists, Labour women could not easily oppose policies which were designed to further the rights and opportunities of the working classes. But often these policies entailed an emphasis on the rights of the working *man*, rather than the working *woman*. For example, as unemployment rose after the First World War, the trade unions, who were key supporters of the Labour Party, understandably sought to defend the interests of their members first. Women were the first group to be sacrificed in the effort to protect men's jobs (see pages 55–6). Thus the principle that women should have equality of opportunity in employment was not one actively advanced by the Labour Party.

Many suffragists became highly disillusioned, especially when the Labour government failed to promote policies that were specifically feminist. The Six Point Group, a women's organisation founded by Lady Rhondda, which campaigned for political and economic equality, was most disenchanted with Labour politicians, such as

MacDonald, Henderson and Snowden, who had previously demon-strated pro-feminist sympathies, but did nothing to encourage appro-priate policies when in power. Labour's dilatory approach to equal suffrage reflected not only an innate male bias, but also a real fear of the consequences of creating a female majority within the electorate.

Nevertheless, Labour was anxious to attract the new women voters. Dr. Marion Phillips was the chief woman organiser within the Women's Sections and had the responsibility of increasing the number of female members and of promoting the Labour Party. Yet Phillips discouraged links with the non-party women's organisations such as the WCA because they were regarded as being middle-class and opposed to class politics. The difficulty therefore for women socialists was whether to support an organisation which represented their gender or one which expounded class solidarity. Although sup-port for both was possible, those who joined the Labour Party were disillusioned on so many occasions by the continuing prevalence of male traditionalism and class politics.

c) The Conservative Party

Despite a traditional reluctance amongst many Conservatives to enfranchise women, leading Conservatives did appreciate the import-ant electoral significance of a new source of party support. Their eventual acceptance of the 30 year old age limit in the 1918 Act, and their preference during the 1920s for the proposed reduction in age limit to 25 years, was based on the belief that older women, especially married women, would probably vote Conservative, unlike the more unpredictable younger, single women.

The Conservatives did not face the same dilemmas as Labour regarding women's role within their party. Traditionally, women had remained on the periphery of the party, their function being support-ive rather than decision-making. During the 1920s, the party sensed the need to establish a more concrete relationship with Conservative women's organisations, but they were prevented from influencing policies. Thus groups such as the women's sections of the Primrose League, an organisation for rank and file Conservatives, and the Women's Unionist Organisation (WUO), founded in 1918, were incorporated within the structure of the National Union of Conservative Associations and permitted to have representatives on the Executive. In 1926, Dame Caroline Bridgeman became the first woman chairperson of the National Union and was the first woman chair of any political party. The Conservatives accepted quite readily the administrative skills and expertise of their women supporters but, as has been evident throughout the twentieth century, were notably hesitant in appointing women to key political office.

Nevertheless, Conservative women were a forceful and effective com-ponent within the party. Middle-class women had time to undertake unpaid political work because so few of them were in paid employment. The strong tradition established in the late nineteenth century of providing a social forum for women was enhanced so that women were now prominent speakers, campaigners and mobilisers of local party support. At annual party conferences they took to the platform and debated motions of national importance such as Ireland. The main legacy of the efforts to attract more women to the Conservative Party was the fact that the party acquired a solid membership which backed the domestic-orientated policies advanced by successive Conservative governments after 1918.

6 Women in Local Government

> **KEY ISSUE** Why were women attracted to local government?

For many women, local government offered a more fulfilling career than national politics. Women had long been involved in local government, sitting on School Boards, Public Health Committees and Poor Law Boards. Single women ratepayers had been enfranchised since 1869. Thus women had actively contributed to the affairs of their local community, often applying their expertise in family welfare issues, well before they could participate in national affairs. Although the ability to vote in general elections and to stand for Parliament widened women's political horizons, many preferred to remain in local government where they thought they could be most effective.

Local government offered many advantages. It avoided, for married women at least, the problems of life in Westminster and the corresponding strain on an individual's family. It was easier, for example, to arrange childcare when working locally rather than in London. Fighting a local election, where they might be more of a familiar figure to the electorate, was less daunting than competing in a large parliamentary constituency. Often, women were already well-known for their work on local committees. Standing as a local councillor seemed the next progressive step. Edith Summerskill typified that pattern, having gained her local expertise first as a co-opted member of the Maternity and Child Welfare Committee in Wood Green (she had trained as a doctor), as well as accompanying and making speeches on behalf of the local Labour candidate for Tottenham and Harringay. Shortly thereafter she was asked to stand for the Green Lane ward in Harringay. In her autobiography she noted that her campaign focused largely on social issues, the perception being that she could speak with most authority on those subjects.

Hannah Mitchell had similar experiences. As a local councillor she served on the Baths and Public Health, Libraries and Parks Committees as well as giving a spirited defence of the rights of married women, especially teachers, to be employed. Although both

Summerskill and Mitchell encountered predictable opposition from men who believed that women should remain in the home, their success as councillors was replicated across the country. In 1919, 121 women alone were elected to the London County Council.

In 1929 women's participation in local government was undermined by the Local Government Act, which removed the Boards of Guardians and replaced them with Public Assistance Committees. Formerly, women had been elected as Poor Law Guardians, now they had to be co-opted which meant that membership was by invitation only. But they now encountered the on-going reluctance of men to include women in local government. Consequently, NUSEC called for a renewed effort in 1929 to get more women elected as councillors – otherwise the chance to influence local affairs would be lost. However, although women's achievements in local government surpassed those in national politics, they never attained more than 5 to 6 per cent of the total of local government councillors during the inter-war years. Despite the fact that women were the majority of the electorate (52.7 per cent in 1929), their numbers in local government remained disproportionately low.

7 Conclusion

> **KEY ISSUE** What were the political advances made by women between the wars?

Between 1918 and 1939 women had hoped to realise political equality with men. They were able to claim partial success in that women were accorded the same voting rights as men in 1928. But they failed to gain their fair share of representation in the Commons. What should a 'fair share' have been? As women were a majority of the electorate, should they have gained at least half the seats in the Commons? Or should it have been in proportion to the number of votes women cast? The fact that women stood no chance of acquiring fair representation certainly strengthened the argument of those who believed in proportional representation. The immediate impact, however, of only a handful of women MPs in Parliament meant that their ability to affect government policies was severely diminished.

The effect of the vote on women was not as dramatic as anti-suffragists had feared. Women were keen to exercise their political rights, but their vote did not revolutionise the nature of British politics. Labour had emerged as the second largest party regardless of the women's vote. If anything, women tended to vote for the Conservatives during the inter-war years. What disappointed feminists was the fact that, despite having an opportunity to press for equal opportunities, women allowed their political attitudes to be shaped by male-directed trends in national politics. The vote may have been

instrumental in persuading governments of the importance of implementing welfare reforms for the family (see pages 63–4), but it was
not applied as a powerful tool to ensure equality.

This failure was compounded by the fact that the majority of male
politicians had no desire to implement equality. Although attitudes
within Parliament were respectful to women, women were not
accorded special treatment. Women had to compete with men for
selection as parliamentary candidates, and contend with in-built bias
towards their sex. The fact that historically they had so many disadvantages compared with men was not an issue which could be quickly
rectified. Not surprisingly, therefore, women continued to encounter
enormous problems in pursuing a political career.

However, it is important to retain a balanced perspective on what
women achieved. If we were to judge success solely according the cri-
terion of how many women entered parliament, it could be argued that
there was little to celebrate. But if we compare women's achievements
with those of newly enfranchised groups of men in the nineteenth century, their achievements in terms of legislation affecting women and
their involvement in national and local politics become far more commendable. Women possessed the potential to effect change directly, to
shape policies so that, as will be seen in Chapter 4, government thinking did respond more positively to the issues that concerned women.

References

1 *The Vote*, 6 December 1918, vol.xviii, no.476, p.4 (Fawcett Library).
2 Quoted in Christopher Sykes, *Nancy, the Life of Lady Astor* (Collins, 1972),
  p. 190.
3 Brian Harrison, *Prudent Revolutionaries: Portraits of British Feminists between
  the Wars* (Clarendon Press, 1987), p. 132.
4 Quoted in Martin Pugh, *Women and the Women's Movement in Britain
  1914–1959* (Macmillan, 1992), p. 149.
5 Thelma Cazalet-Keir, *From the Wings* (The Bodley Head, 1967), p. 126.
6 Edith Summerskill, *A Woman's World* (Heinemann, 1967), p. 61–2.
7 Parliamentary Debates, vol.125, 27 February 1920, col. 2068.
8 *Ibid.*, col. 2078.
9 NUSEC Annual Report 1919 (Box 342, GB/106/2/NUSEC/C2, Fawcett
  Library), p. 13.
10 NUSEC, *The Case for Equal Franchise*, 1925.
11 Cheryl Law, *Suffrage and Power: the Women's Movement 1918–1928* (I.B.
  Tauris., 1997), p. 213.

Summary Diagram
Political Advances in the Inter-War Years

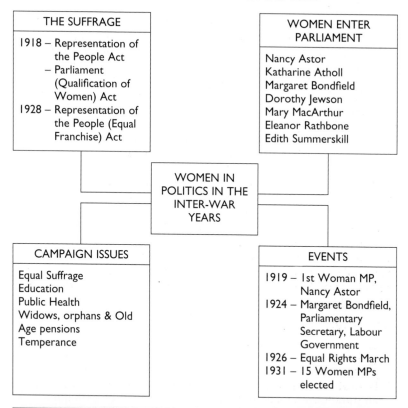

THE SUFFRAGE

1918 – Representation of
    the People Act
  – Parliament
    (Qualification of
    Women) Act
1928 – Representation of
    the People (Equal
    Franchise) Act

WOMEN ENTER
PARLIAMENT

Nancy Astor
Katharine Atholl
Margaret Bondfield
Dorothy Jewson
Mary MacArthur
Eleanor Rathbone
Edith Summerskill

WOMEN IN
POLITICS IN THE
INTER-WAR
YEARS

CAMPAIGN ISSUES

Equal Suffrage
Education
Public Health
Widows, orphans & Old
Age pensions
Temperance

EVENTS

1919 – 1st Woman MP,
    Nancy Astor
1924 – Margaret Bondfield,
    Parliamentary
    Secretary, Labour
    Government
1926 – Equal Rights March
1931 – 15 Women MPs
    elected

Working on Chapter 3

You should now have a checklist which identifies the main political
gains and setbacks incurred by women in the inter-war years. Make sure
that your list refers to women as a whole as well as particular individuals.

Now use this list as a guideline for a more detailed assessment of
women's progress during these years. Make notes analysing the questions raised in the Key Issues boxes for each section of the chapter.
You should evaluate the questions from two angles: i) the extent to
which women themselves were effecting change and ii) the role, positive or otherwise, played by governments and political parties. It will
be important to examine changing attitudes amongst both women
and men as well as the way new policies towards women evolved. By
the end of your note-making, you should not only be able to explain
how women advanced politically between the wars, but also why. You
should also be able to explain the reasons for their limited impact on
British politics.

Answering structured questions on Chapter 3

Look at the following questions:

1. Women in Parliament

a) Why were women so unsuccessful in getting any women MPs elected to Parliament in December 1918? (*5 marks*)

b) Explain why so few women entered Parliament during the inter-war years. (*10 marks*)

c) How effective were women as MPs between the wars? (*15 marks*)

2. The Campaign for Equal Franchise

a) What were the main arguments deployed by women in support of equal franchise? (*5 marks*)

b) Why were the main political parties reluctant to introduce equal franchise legislation? (*10 marks*)

c) How significant was external pressure in influencing the decision to introduce equal suffrage? (*15 marks*)

Hints and advice: These questions are designed to test your understanding of causation and your ability to judge and analyse the relative importance of certain key issues. Question 1 looks at the progress of women in politics between the wars. Both parts a) and b) require you to examine the reasons for women's lack of success in entering Parliament. For part a), however, you need to focus quite specifically on short-term reasons for failure. Points to consider might be the particular circumstances in which that election was fought. You should try to explain each reason carefully, demonstrating the extent to which it helps to answer the question. In addition, you might find it helpful to recall some of the ideas you considered when reading Chapter 2. Do these ideas help you to provide more of an overall explanation for the results of 1918? Part b) is a little more complex because there will be a number of interacting causal factors which will have to be examined. Attitudes – of women, men, members of political parties – will be one vital topic to explore. But whatever reasons you give, be sure to explain how important you consider these points in relation to the question.

Questions 1c) and 2c) are phrased using the terms either 'how effective' or 'how significant'? With these questions you have to think about the degree to which something was effective or significant. This means you have to evaluate the relative importance of, for example, external pressure and compare this with other factors that may have helped to bring about equal franchise. This kind of argument might need to assess strengths and weaknesses of a viewpoint; it will certainly require a balanced answer, one which has explored other contributory factors as well.

Further essay questions

1. Why did women fail to establish a Women's Party between the wars?

2. How did the arguments in favour of women's suffrage change between 1918 and 1928?

4 Economic and Social Change, 1918–39

POINTS TO CONSIDER

In conjunction with the previous chapter, Chapter 4 continues the evaluation of the inter-war years and seeks to establish the extent to which women experienced further economic and social emancipation after the conclusion of the First World War. If, as was suggested in Chapter 1, the First World War was one of many catalysts for change during the twentieth century, were the apparent advances in women's status within society between 1914 and 1918 sustained or not? Your preliminary reading of the chapter should enable you to appreciate the factors shaping the role of women in society between 1918 and 1939 but should also leave you posing further questions as to how and why such developments occurred.

KEY DATES

1918		*Married Love and Wise Parenthood* published.
	Mar	Trade union resolutions on women's post-war employment.
		Fisher Education Act.
	11 Nov	Armistice.
1918–19		Large-scale dismissal of women from wartime jobs.
1919		Sex Discrimination (Removal) Act.
	June	Pre-War Trade Practices Act.
1920		*Time and Tide* founded by Lady Rhondda.
		Unemployment Insurance Act.
1921		The Six Point Group established.
		First Marie Stopes birth control clinic opened.
1922		Criminal Law Amendment Act.
1923		Matrimonial Causes Act.
1924		*The Disinherited Family* published.
1925		Guardianship of Infants Act.
		Widows, Orphans and Old Age Contributory Pensions Act.
1926		Hadow Report on Education.
1927		Legitimacy Act.
		NUSEC executive split; resignation of equality feminists.
1928		Equal Franchise Act.
1931		Unemployment (Anomalies) Act.

1 Introduction

> **KEY ISSUE** What were the factors which proved crucial in determining the direction of women's economic and social role in Britain after 1918?

Both Chapters 2 and 3 established the fact that the First World War was a facilitator of change for women. Politically, there was no turning back. Equal franchise was finally attained in 1928 and although advances thereafter were scarcely dramatic, the potential for exerting further influence in politics had been created. The pressures of war had also challenged the conventional status of women, instigating less economic dependency on men as well as greater social freedoms. But did the return to peace signal the end of such progress, or were women able to capitalise on their wartime experiences and secure a greater degree of economic and social independence?

Although the full effects of returning to a peacetime economy could not have been predicted, women were immediate victims of the upheaval arising from demobilisation, the upsurge in unemployment and a reversion to pre-war trade practices. In particular, women frequently discovered that they were expected either to revert to traditional forms of employment or accept less prominent, lower paid jobs than those held by men. Yet whilst some women appeared to tolerate and even support the principle that it was the man's prerogative to earn a living wage, other women sought to retain newly-gained economic and social rights. Thus by 1939, important developments regarding the nature of female employment and the wider role of women in society had occurred. What is important to ascertain is the extent to which those developments constituted a change or, basically, continuity with the past.

Government legislation was another instrumental factor in affecting women's role in society. An interesting question to examine, therefore, is whether in initiating political reform, governments genuinely supported female emancipation, or whether they had a different, more limited agenda for women when determining policies. Why, for example, did so much of the legislation passed by inter-war governments focus on reforming the rights of women within the family, but do so little to guarantee real equality of opportunity or equal pay?

Finally, women's own perceptions of what role they should exercise in post-war Britain was of fundamental importance in either promoting or restricting the emancipation of women. Women's groups had sustained a remarkable momentum of campaigning for women's rights since long before the First World War. The programme of unfinished business was extensive, as now women sought to clarify the issues which would shape their future roles in society. But dissension and disagreement amongst leading individuals reflected a profound schism in feminist ideology, with differing views prevailing over whether there should be emphasis on assisting women to stay at home or to seek parity with men. The causes and effects of these divisions provide a central explanation for both the nature and pace of change concerning women during the inter-war years.

2 The Return to a Peacetime Economy

> **KEY ISSUES** How were women affected by the return to a peacetime economy? Which was greater, the change or continuity in work practices after the end of the war, and were the results for the better or worse?

a) The Immediate Problems of the Post-war Economy

i) Unemployment

During the war, women had proved themselves to be an essential component of the nation's workforce, with over 4.5 million employed in industry (see pages 18–19). Nevertheless, although women's contributions to the war effort were highly praised, undercurrents of opposition to female employment had persisted. In the Treasury Agreement of 1915, the government had conceded to the trade unions that dilution of labour would terminate once the war ended. In March 1918, a male-dominated trade union conference passed specific resolutions regarding the future employment of women in industry, recommending a reduction in the working day from 12 to eight hours, with just four hours on a Saturday. The assumption was that industrial work for married women was incompatible with the demands of family life. In June 1919, any remaining hopes amongst women's groups such as the Women's Freedom League that advances made in skilled jobs would be sustained after 1918 were thwarted by the enactment of the Pre-War Trade Practices Act. This finalised the terms set out in the Treasury Agreement and so guaranteed a return to pre-war working conditions for women. By 1921, the female industrial workforce had been reduced to a level two per cent lower than that in 1914.

Fears amongst women's groups that jobs would be eroded once the war ended were well founded. The government had to oversee the demobilisation of three and a half million men with the result that women were soon faced with unemployment. In just two weeks after the conclusion of the war, 113,000 women were dismissed from jobs in industry, and by April 1919 600,000 were unemployed.[1] The Woolwich Arsenal, which had been the largest employer of women munitions workers, dismissed a total of 25,000, with 6,000 leaving in November 1918 alone. Those women reacted to a paltry seven shillings (35p) a week unemployment benefit by marching in protest in London. One of the banners bore the message, 'Shall Peace bring in Starvation'.[2] In transport, where women had successfully undertaken men's jobs on the railways, buses and trams, women were replaced by men, whilst those who retained their posts for a while were sharply criticised for doing a 'man's job'. Similar dismissals occurred in the skilled engineering jobs despite women's accomplished contributions.

As pressure mounted to soften the blows of unemployment, the government established the 'out-of-work' donation scheme whereby women got 25s (£1 22.5p) a week for 13 weeks, on condition that they attended the labour exchange every day and were available for work. By November 1919, the rate had been reduced to 15s (75p) a week. In 1920, the economic slump commenced and the rates of unemployment amongst women rose more rapidly than for men. The Unemployment Insurance Act 1920, did nothing to ease women's situation. It replaced the 'out-of-work' scheme and limited benefits to 12s (60p) a week, a rate lower than that for men. The stipulation that women had to accept offers of work was much resented as a refusal led to benefits being withdrawn (see page 58). As a result, the number of women claiming benefits became almost negligible. Married women were most adversely affected as they were only eligible for benefits if they had paid National Insurance stamps before the war.

ii) Employment and the Marriage Bar

The government's attitude towards fostering female employment differed sharply from that displayed during the war. The only positive effort was a donation of half a million pounds in 1920 to the Central Committee for Women's Training and Employment which established training centres in horticulture, hairdressing, journalism and domestic work. However, by 1921, only the last of these occupations received any support.

The strains of establishing a peacetime economy had repercussions not only for women industrial workers but also for the thousands of women in clerical and other non-industrial jobs. During the war, women had sustained the pre-war trend of gaining work in the Civil Service to the extent that 56 per cent of civil service employees were women, although many of the posts were reserved for returning ex-servicemen. Yet in a reorganisation of the Civil Service in 1919 experienced female civil servants who had taken professional exams were replaced by unqualified, inexperienced male employees. Furthermore, women were segregated and allocated to lower grade positions, thus consigning them to routine and monotonous clerical work. For many ensuing decades, women's contribution to the Civil Service was largely confined to the repetitive tasks of the typing pool, whilst men rose through the ranks to positions of authority.

The failure to implement fully the terms of the Sex Discrimination (Removal) Act of 1919 was another setback. The Act had seemed to be a victory for further female emancipation as it prohibited 'disqualifying a person from the exercise of any public function or appointment because of sex or marital status'.[3] Women could no longer be barred from entering the professions such as law, medicine or the Civil Service and certainly the 1920s and 1930s witnessed a slow but steady increase in women seeking professional careers. Despite government pledges that in principle women should be able to compete equally with men in qualifying for the Civil Service, by stipulating that certain posts should be reserved for ex-servicemen, they ensured that women were disadvantaged in comparison.

Other employers of public servants soon managed to circumvent the Sex Discrimination (Removal) Act. In a test case it was ruled that married women could be barred from teaching as married women were not necessarily entitled to employment. This set a precedent for the 1920s and 1930s. London introduced a marriage bar for all teachers in 1923, and by 1926 some 75 per cent of all local authorities had imposed restrictions on the employment of married women. Doctors, nurses and other health workers were also dismissed as soon as they got married. This discrimination was a bitter pill to swallow so shortly after the inclusion of married women over the age of 30 on the electoral register. The expectations that such women had now gained the respect of their male counterparts had proven false. As the Women's Freedom League noted in 1923:

1 We know that the presence of women among the law-makers and administrators has caused a very considerable change, and we must see to it that more women are elected in the near future. Meanwhile women are being persecuted and victimised not for inefficiency, but
5 because of their sex or because they are married.[4]

The marriage bar in the Home Civil Service was not abolished until 1946, although the London County Council ended its marriage bar against teachers, doctors and nurses in 1935.

iii) Women and their Role in the Nation's Economy

Did these setbacks to women's employment set the trend for the post-war years or did women's economic roles make some advances? The tendency for women to leave work once they were married continued, whether this was instigated by government policies, trade union intransigence to female employment or the attitudes of women themselves (see Section 4). After the war, the number of working married women aged 25 and over dropped whilst the overall proportion of married women working stayed consistent with pre-war levels of around ten per cent.

Marital Status	Year	15–24	25–34	35–44	45–54	55 and over
Single	1911	73.05	73.59	65.61	58.53	34.48
	1931	75.73	80.41	72.37	63.90	36.38
Married	1911	12.00	9.92	9.93	9.92	7.20
	1931	18.50	13.19	10.16	8.51	5.32

Female participation rates by age and marital status – Great Britain, 1911 and 1931 (percentages)[5]

Only in the age group of 18–24 did numbers increase slightly by about five per cent, most probably because those women had yet to start a family. For single women, work opportunities declined as they grew older, although men were less affected by this problem. Thus the typical woman worker during the inter-war years tended to be young and single – 69 per cent of the female workforce in 1931 was under the age of 35.

After 1918, domestic service remained the largest source of employment for women, although for those used to the better pay and greater independence associated with many wartime jobs, the return to a life of isolation and servitude was not welcome. Women increasingly opposed the rigid rules, uniform, long hours and the overall exploitation of what was seen as an underclass of society. In 1918, though, the dearth of servants caused an enormous outcry resulting in government promotion of domestic service as a 'useful' and 'worthwhile' occupation. Training courses under the auspices of the Central Committee on Women's Training and Employment were set up and even received the official endorsement of the Women's Trade Union League. However, the notion that women were content to return to a job characterised by low pay, lack of independence and the need for deference undermined so much of what women had achieved between 1914 and 1918. Unemployed women also risked losing benefits if they rejected offers of work, even if the only jobs available were in domestic service. One woman in Newcastle, who was a member of the National Federation of Women Workers, refused to accept domestic work at six shillings (30p) a week, and so was deprived of further benefits. Despite the fact that recruitment to the training courses was poor, domestic service continued to be promoted, not least during the Depression when, in 1931 for example, 16 non-residential courses in domestic service were established in the north-east alone. Overall, some 35 per cent of all working women were in domestic service in 1931.

The reduction in the percentage of women employed in traditional industries proved to be a long-term consequence of the return to a peacetime economy. The textile and clothing trade – the second largest source of employment after domestic service – was badly affected by a post-war slump, and further aggravated by the onset of the Depression in 1929. For those in employment, wage reductions were an additional threat. The Yorkshire woollen trade, with a 60 per cent female workforce, was subjected to frequent wage cuts in 1930 which, despite protest strikes, were successfully implemented. Similarly in the Lancashire cotton industry, where some towns were already experiencing 50 per cent unemployment, employers undercut wage agreements and instigated work practices favouring men. Foreign competition also decimated traditional female employment such as dressmaking, millinery and tailoring, reducing the numbers employed from pre-war levels of approximately 406,000 to around 280,000 in England and Wales in 1931.[6] Another typical source of employment, outworkers and homeworkers (see page 4), likewise declined.

Amongst middle-class women there was a growing expectation that they should seek a professional career, but despite the passing of the Sex Discrimination (Removal) Act, opportunities were limited. In the legal profession, for example, 77 women had succeeded in becoming barristers by 1926. But in medicine, the number of women entering the profession only increased from six per cent in 1911 to 7.5 per cent during the inter-war years. The practice adopted by most London hospitals during the war of admitting women as students and registrars ceased after 1919, with the exception of University College Hospital and The Royal Free Hospital. In teaching and nursing, the numbers declined from 63 per cent to 59 per cent over a similar period.[7] Despite the fact that teaching was increasingly perceived as an attractive career for middle-class women, the impact of the marriage bar undoubtedly had a detrimental effect on total numbers.

Some trends, however, were not reversed or checked. The post-war period witnessed a continued expansion in the numbers of women employed in shopkeeping and clerical work, with the latter experiencing an increase of 694 per cent from the 1911 level by 1931. A high proportion of women were retained in banking and accounting, although they were often relegated to the more routine jobs, as indeed had occurred in the Civil Service. Those women who broke through the lower ranks were the exception. Between 1931 and 1934, 40 women sat the Home Civil Service exams but not one was successful. When one candidate, Jennifer Hart, passed the exam in 1936, coming third out of a total of 493, her success 'created an enormous sensation'.[8] Evidently, few women possessed the confidence to seek posts of responsibility. But those who did faced huge obstacles in convincing male employers that they were capable of doing 'male' work.

New opportunities emerged in the south-east and midlands where the growth in light industries deploying mass production on assembly lines provided jobs for women. A common characteristic of jobs in industries like food production and the making of electrical appliances was the fact that skills were less at a premium than the ability to cope with repetitive and monotonous tasks such as wiring radios or filling up boxes of chocolates. Employers deemed women more suitable than men to undertake such work because their labour was cheap and their fingers regarded as more dextrous. Thus important long-term trends were established in the inter-war years whereby women dominated the less-skilled sections of industry but would usually leave employment once they got married.

Finally, another factor which concerned women's involvement in the nation's economy was the continuing differentials relating to pay and unemployment benefits between men and women. In this respect, little had changed since before the war. On average, in both industrial and non-industrial work, women's wages were 50 per cent lower than those of men. Discrimination applied equally elsewhere. In 1920 and 1921, resolutions were passed in the House of Commons urging equal pay in the Civil Service. In 1936, Ellen Wilkinson successfully secured a motion in favour of common salary scales for men and women, but Baldwin, the Prime Minister, 'turned it into a vote of no confidence and the decision was reversed'.[9] By insisting that women were graded separately, the Civil Service had ensured that women were paid differently from men.

The policy on unemployment benefits for women continued to be prejudiced against women, notably those who were married. In 1931, a determined cohort of women MPs – Eleanor Rathbone, Jennie Lee, Ellen Wilkinson and Cynthia Mosley – unsuccessfully fought the proposed Unemployment (Anomalies) Bill, introduced by a fellow female MP, Margaret Bondfield, Minister of Labour in the Labour government, which made it even more difficult for married women to claim benefits, even if they had paid contributions. Under the act which passed, a married woman leaving the labour market, perhaps to have children, was classified as having retired and therefore no longer eligible for benefits.

What emerges from the issues discussed so far is that women's economic role in society continued to reflect familiar underlying trends, despite the interruption of the First World War. A number of factors militated against the employment of married women, whilst those who did work, whether married or single, experienced discrimination in terms of pay and status of jobs. Those women who entered the professions remained in a minority, those working in clerical jobs were usually confined to the lower grades, and those in industry to the more routine, less skilled tasks. Where new employment opportunities emerged, employers invariably ensured that men, rather than women, were granted the more prestigious jobs.

3 Government Policies towards Women

KEY ISSUE What were the principles which determined government policies towards women in the inter-war years?

a) A Pragmatic Response to a Practical Problem?

The effects of restoring Britain's economy after the upheaval of the war had had a dramatic impact on female employment. What needs to be understood, however, is the paradox of a government which had granted the vote to women yet then denied them the chance of pursuing economic equality. What were the motives, therefore, of governments in the post-war period regarding their approach to women's economic and social role in society?

In 1918, the government faced the practical problems of how to ease the transition from a war-time to a peace-time economy. This challenge was exacerbated by the fact that the government had a sense of obligation both to the demobilised soldiers who had sacrificed so much during the war, and the trade unions who had waived traditional working practices. Faced with the urgent need to re-employ several million men, the government looked to women to vacate their jobs without too much protest.

Government policy clearly reflected the low priority given both to women's employment and those unemployed. Only limited assistance was offered by the Women's Employment Committee of the Ministry of Reconstruction established in 1919. The Committee offered guidance on women's employment, although the hope was expressed that 'every inducement, direct or indirect, will be given to keep mothers at home'.[10] The fact that the only effective government training scheme was for domestic service suggests a clear government policy towards women's employment.

Recognition of the concessions made by trade unions regarding dilution of labour during the war also influenced the government's approach to women's employment. Such co-operation had been welcome, but now trade union expectations on jobs had to be met. In addition, the government's problems were compounded as the economic crisis deepened. The retraction in traditional areas of employment, which was further exacerbated by the Depression, forced the government to make unpopular decisions regarding British industries, especially coal. They had enough problems placating the unions without aggravating the problem by actively protecting female employment.

The government could also take comfort from the fact that national opinion was firmly in favour of women vacating their jobs for returning servicemen. Women, especially those who were married, who remained in their jobs, were accused of being opportunist, denying men their rightful place as the chief breadwinner again. It was a sharp reversal from the praiseworthy tones of the national press towards women's patriotism in the war.

b) Ideology

The reactions outlined above cannot be understood purely in terms of a pragmatic response to an immediate economic crisis or even the more serious problems arising from the Depression of 1929. Such policies may have been a convenient tactic given the problems of coping with the post-war situation, but a more subtle and convincing argument was needed if such policies were to be sustained. Thus the government's attitude towards women's role in society during the inter-war years was guided by a very definite ideology which determined the nature of their policies. In many respects the essential beliefs underlying this philosophy were consistent with pre-war thinking, only now they were expressed more explicitly. One prominent idea was the belief that a woman's most important function was that of reproduction. Her primary responsibilities in life were to her family and the upbringing of children. Secondly, the natural corollary to women being at home was that developing a set of skills with which to compete in the labour market became of secondary importance. Hence it was acceptable to implement sexual segregation in the workplace, with women undertaking less skilled work because they were not expected to become primary wage-earners.

c) The Implications of Government Policies

What further evidence is there that the government sought to encourage an agenda of domestication, of encouraging women to stay in the home? A survey of some of the legislation affecting women passed by governments during the 1920s reveals a strong emphasis on promoting women's roles as wives and mothers. In one respect it could be argued that the government was responding to feminist concerns. Often the legislation was designed to counteract discrimination against women, such as the Matrimonial Causes Act of 1923 which permitted a wife to divorce her husband on grounds of adultery, a right previously denied by the Divorce Act of 1857. Similarly, the Guardianship of Infants Act, 1925, granted limited concessions to feminist demands for equal guardianship for mothers by permitting equal parental rights to children once a dispute went to court. Yet government tactics over this bill symbolised a consistent approach to women's issues. When the Guardianship of Infants Bill as supported by the NUSEC seemed likely to be debated in the Commons, the government reacted by introducing its own, more moderate bill. A similar principle applied to the Widows, Orphans and Old Age Contributory Pensions Act of 1925 which recognised the importance of giving widows financial protection but restricted its provisions to women whose children were under 14 and a half years old on the basis that these children were still probably at school.

Other legislation addressed some of the moral standards inherited from the Victorians, such as the Criminal Law Amendment Act of 1922, which raised the age of consent for girls from thirteen to sixteen, and the Legitimacy Act of 1927 which, following campaigns by the National Council for the Unmarried Mother and her Child, legitimised a child when its parents got married. Thus the stigma of illegitimacy was removed, although only if couples conformed to the principles of marriage.

Nevertheless, underlying motives were clear. All the political parties shared a concern to facilitate women's domestic duties and responsibilities as well as protecting children and young girls. These acts carried the accolade of being morally virtuous, but did little to undermine men's roles as heads of household or family breadwinner. Feminists were often disappointed by the limitations of the reforms, but at the same time reluctant to obstruct any proposed legislation. Amongst non-feminists, however, there was little inclination to challenge the trend of domestication. Traditional attitudes were perpetuated by the combination of educational policies, the realities of limited employment opportunities and cultural expectations of women.

d) Education

Educational policies provide further insights into how both government and society viewed the role of women. In 1918, the Fisher Education Act instituted full-time education for both boys and girls in free, public elementary schools up to the age of 14. This was followed by the Hadow Report in 1926 which recommended the separation of education into two sectors, primary up to 11 years, and secondary from 11 to 14. The problem with the latter was that these schools were fee-paying. Thus for working-class children the options were either to remain in the overcrowded elementary schools, or compete for a free-place in the secondary school, a benefit restricted to just seven per cent of all children.

For girls, the quality of education received depended totally on class and income. Working-class girls had little choice but to leave school at 14. At elementary school, the emphasis was on the three 'Rs', some humanities and domestic economy. Indeed, domestic science was encouraged by the Board of Education on the grounds that working-class women needed a sound knowledge of nutrition and hygiene. Thousands of girls attended cookery centres, as well as maternity and infant welfare clinics. Implicit in such policies was the view that girls should be well prepared for the challenges of motherhood.

For more privileged girls whose parents could afford fees, there were greater opportunities to have an academic education. It was within the all-female establishments of the private schools that girls most successfully challenged narrow perceptions regarding their future roles. Schools such as those under the auspices of the Girls' Public Day School Trust encouraged their pupils to seek a professional career, training them to sit the School Certificate at 16, the Higher School Certificate at 18 and to apply to university. Figures for university attendance amongst women show a steady increase during the inter-war years, although the extent to which these qualifications were utilised must have been affected by attitudes such as the resistance to the employment of married women. Above all, those women benefiting from either a decent secondary or university education were in a minority. For the majority, school was a short prelude before entering the world of work and domestic responsibilities.

4 The Feminist Response

> **KEY ISSUE** Why did divisions occur within the feminist movement during the inter-war years and what implications did these disagreements have for the evolving role of women within society?

a) New Feminism Versus Equality Feminism

In 1918 there appeared to be a consensus amongst women's groups that, having acquired a limited franchise for women, they should now aim not only for complete political but also social and economic equality. Whereas the government was quietly hoping that agitation on women's issues would recede, women were outlining future policy objectives. Hopes focused on securing the election to Parliament of women who would then shift the balance of the typical political agenda towards enacting issues that affected women. In particular, there were expectations that reforms on maternity and child welfare, equal guardianship of children, housing, education, widows' pensions and children's allowances would be implemented. Above all, there were vociferous demands for equal pay, equality of opportunity and equal moral standards, whereby men as well as women would become liable to prosecution in cases of immoral behaviour.

Optimism was soon tempered by the realities of post-war politics. The disappointing performance of women candidates in the 1918 election reinforced the determination of women's organisations to lobby and campaign outside Parliament. But strong ideological differences emerged amongst feminists which had been partly submerged by the exigencies of war. The arguments centred on whether women's needs were different from those of men, as advocated by the 'New Feminists', or whether women should seek complete equality with men on the grounds that they should be treated no differently to men, a view propounded by the 'Equality Feminists'.

New feminism represented the more moderate wing of the women's movement in the inter-war years. Its supporters believed in a woman-centred approach to women's issues, claiming that women had particular needs which had to be addressed by specific legislation. A system of family allowances such as payments to support children would enable women to remain in the home, rather than seek lowly paid work. This approach reiterated the importance of women's roles as wives and mothers yet also advocated the need to safeguard women from neglect and ill-treatment.

The emphasis on women's roles as wives and mothers met with sharp criticism from equality feminists who, even during the First World War, had believed that women should campaign for equal rights with men. These ideas were encouraged by new feminist interpretations of history, most notably Alice Clark's *Working Life of Women in the Seventeenth Century* (1919) which saw:

> women's exclusion from production as the root cause of their oppression in public life, underlying and making possible 'the organisation of a State which regards the purposes of life solely from the male standpoint'.[11]

This exposition of the erosion in the status of women appealed to the equality feminists who believed that only with true economic, social and political emancipation could women escape from the ties of a patriarchal society.

b) The Feminist Campaigns

i) Employment, Family Allowances and Equal Pay

In the years immediately after the end of the First World War, resolutions demanding equal pay and equal opportunities were passed regularly by the NUSEC, the Women's Freedom League (WFL), and endorsed by organisations such as the Federation of Women's Civil Servants (FWCS), the Women's Industrial League (WIL), founded in 1918, and the National Union of Women Teachers (NUWT). Close co-operation prevailed between these and many other organisations in order to present a united front to the government. Both the Annual Conferences of the NUSEC and the WFL repeatedly criticised the government for failing to remove existing inequalities, despite election pledges to address such issues. The WFL also attacked trade unions for deliberately opposing women's interests, charging them with waging a sex-war against female employment. Support was given to teachers and civil servants as they fought to gain equal pay.

In principle, therefore, as job opportunities for women retracted, there was a consensus that efforts must be sustained to protect female employment. But although there appeared to be a universal subscription to an equal rights policy, there were differences in interpretation as to how it should be implemented. In particular, it was the focus on protective legislation for women which proved so divisive within the feminist movement.

These arguments were most powerfully articulated by Eleanor Rathbone, who had founded the Family Endowment Society in 1917 and was subsequently President of the NUSEC from 1919 to 1928. In 1924 Rathbone published *The Disinherited Family* which was one of several key feminist works to emerge during the inter-war years. In her book, she outlined her main theories on the need for welfare legislation. First, she identified the problem of the 'family wage', contending that wages were insufficient to meet the needs of most working-class families. Rathbone calculated that large numbers of men earned less than what was deemed to be the minimum level necessary to support a family. This had serious implications for women who were often forced to supplement the inadequate family income by working for low wages and in poor conditions. Rathbone's second key point was that during the First World War many women and children had benefited from the separate allowances paid to wives of servicemen. This economic independence provided proof of the beneficial effects of welfare legislation since it removed women's dependency on employment or a husband's goodwill to pay a household allowance. Thus a state-run, universal system of allowances could protect women from the dangers of poverty. In addition, she believed that the removal of women from the labour market would assist male efforts to improve wages, as wages would no longer be depressed by the presence of female workers:

1 ... direct provision would result in withdrawing from the labour market
a large proportion of the married women workers, especially those
who only entered it because of the inadequacy of their husbands' earnings ... These have always been unsatisfactory to the employers
5 because of their irregularity, and to their fellow-workers, because they
are impossible to organize and can be easily be forced to take pocket-
money wages.[12]

Rathbone's ideas centred on an acceptance that there were biological
differences between men and women which resulted in different gender
needs and interests. By enhancing women's role as wives and mothers,
Rathbone was reasserting a traditional view of women. In many respects,
her thinking was quite radical, because it gave married women autonomy. It was also closely correlated with more recent thinking on welfare
legislation in that the State was now expected to alleviate the worst of the
economic and social conditions which women had hitherto endured.

Rathbone's views were opposed by feminists such as Ray Strachey,
Ada Nield Chew and Lady Rhondda. Although they agreed with protective legislation, they wanted it applied to both sexes. They opposed
what they considered to be gender differentiation which rendered
women inferior to men. In 1927, the ideological differences resulted
in a serious confrontation within the NUSEC executive, culminating
in a victory by one vote for Rathbone's welfare feminism. As a result,
the equality feminists resigned from the NUSEC executive. Their
actions merely meant that in future feminism was most closely associated with social reform rather than equal rights.

Equality feminists had also opposed family allowances on the grounds
that this would undermine the campaign for equal pay. This was publi-
cised through weekly feminist journals such as *Time and Tide*, founded
by Lady Rhondda in 1920, as well as through another initiative of hers,
the Six Point Group (1921), whose brief was to promote women's equality. They claimed that unless women strove for equal pay and opportunities, their lives would always be directed by a male set of values. Work
should be regarded as a means of emancipating women, not as an intol-
erable burden. If women continued to accept inferior pay and economic
status, their own personal self-development and self-esteem would
always be undermined. Such views were outlined in a letter to *The Times*
in February 1929, in connection with a proposed Factories Bill.

1 The recognition in law of women as adult human beings with the same
personal rights as adult men will be the first step towards correcting
what seems too often to be the assumption that women are permanently inferior workers to be dealt with as a controlled annex to
5 industry. It will be the first step towards the abolition of the present
artificial demarcation between men's work and women's work and
towards the abolition of the unequal wage rates applied to men and
women irrespective of the similarity or even the identity of their work
done.[13]

Despite the strong support for such views amongst many women, by the end of the 1920s equality feminists were no longer a dominant force within the women's movement. As the effects of the Depression deepened, concerns about poverty and its alleviation gained even greater prominence. Differentials between men and women were maintained, thus ensuring that women's role in society remained largely traditional.

ii) The Family and Marriage

During the inter-war period there was a close correlation between differing ideas about women's employment and women's role within the family. As with employment, the question of the family proved contentious, although divisions occurred not only between differing feminist views, but also according to class divides. A growing number of middle-class women disagreed with the ideology which emphasised the vocation of motherhood, believing that marriage should no longer preclude a career. Marriage, they argued, should not be viewed as an economic necessity; rather it should be a partnership which offered companionship.

Middle-class women could afford the luxury of such attitudes. Edith Summerskill recognised that as a doctor, then a politician, her household survived because she had the help of a live-in nanny, Agnes Wakeford, plus a husband who, as another doctor, could come home at lunchtimes. Hannah Mitchell's work as a local councillor was assisted by a domestic help who cooked the family meals. Vera Brittain's partnership with George Catlin epitomised a very modern interpretation of marriage in that the two of them were often separated by continents in their determination to pursue independent careers. Indeed, such women were fortunate they had married men who shared their opinions regarding a woman's autonomy within marriage.

As the marriage bar on employment took effect, the question of what should be women's role within the family became more crucial, especially for those who could not afford to buy extra domestic help. Increasingly, the ideology of marriage and motherhood was subtly but expertly enhanced through a combination of government policies (see Section 3) and the growing popularity of organisations and magazines which focused on women's domestic responsibilities. The combined effect of the Equal Franchise Act of 1928 (see page 44) and the Depression led to a decline in feminism and a revival of traditional views on women's role in the family. Support for the NUSEC fell, whilst organisations such as the Women's Institute and the National Union of Townswomen's Guilds founded in 1932, flourished. The function of these new bodies was to be educational in that they provided a forum in which women could learn the art of public speaking as well as gaining experience in pressure group politics. The issues which predominated, though, were primarily to do with the family, home and motherhood. Worthwhile campaigns were conducted to improve electricity supplies to rural areas, but the motive was one of improving the lot of the woman at home.

As Martin Pugh has demonstrated, the growing success of women's magazines illustrated yet another aspect of what he has described as the 'cult of domesticity'. The rapid expansion in circulation numbers for *Good Housekeeping, Woman's Own, Woman,* and *Woman's Illustrated,* all of which began publishing in the 1930s, indicated the focus on women's domestic roles. Advice on home management was prolific – how to polish your furniture, encouragements to purchase the latest consumer goods such as the Electrolux hoover, expert views on feeding and clothing your baby and how to create the 'modern home', as the advertisement below illustrates.

The October Modern Home (*Woman's Own,* October 15, 1932)

However, for those women who now sought greater independence from family responsibilities, the 'home-making' advice was a complete anathema. As Winfred Holtby, friend of Vera Brittain, wrote in *Women* (1934),

1   It is agreeable to distemper one's own nursery, bake crusts, squeeze
    oranges and mix nourishing salads; it is not agreeable to sit on quar-
    relling committees, listen to tedious speeches, organise demonstrations
    and alter systems, in order that others – for whom such wholesome
5   pleasures are at present impossible – may enjoy them. Yet women are
    praised for the maternal instincts which make the care expended on
    their children natural and pleasant; they are criticised for the political
    activities which result in the safeguarding of other people's children as
    well as their own. So slums remain uncleared, milk is wasted, nursery
10 schools are exceptional luxuries, educational reforms are delayed, while
    'good wives and mothers' shut themselves up in the comforts of their
    private lives and earn the approval of unthinking society.[14]

Further arguments within the feminist movement arose as a result of
increasing public discussion of women' sexuality. By the First World
War a number of writers, for example Stella Browne and Rose
Witcop, had begun to comment more openly on female sexuality by
advocating birth control. Then in 1918, Marie Stopes published
Married Love which, like *The Disinherited Family*, came to symbolise a
major new strand of feminist thought in the inter-war years. Stopes'
book challenged society's traditional perception of sexual relationships by claiming that sex could be enjoyed by women as well as
men.

1   To use a homely simile – one might compare two human beings to two
    bodies charged with electricity of differing potentials. Isolated from each
    other the electric forces within them are invisible, but if they come into
    the right juxtaposition the force is transmuted, and a spark, a glow of
5   burning light arises between them. Such is love.[15]

This rather oblique reference to sexual attraction revealed just how
carefully women like Marie Stopes had to proceed if they wanted their
work to be taken seriously. Too explicit language would have shocked
the intended audience.

In a subsequent book, *Wise Parenthood* (1918), Stopes offered
advice on birth control, advocating the use of 'mechanical devices'
as well as natural methods. Although some basic, artificial means of
birth control already existed, few women had the confidence or
knowledge both to obtain and use such preventative measures.
Stopes gave confidence to thousands of women who could now
contemplate a sexual role other than that of procreation. Stopes'
first birth control clinic opened in Holloway, north London, in
1921 although, as the illustration on page 70 reveals, the early
facilities must have been very basic. By 1930, however, the Ministry
of Health permitted local authorities to offer limited advice on
birth control. Despite opposition from the Roman Catholic
Church, the use of birth control became quite widespread by the
late 1930s.

Pioneer Birth Control Caravan of the 1920s

Within the feminist movement, there was considerable support for birth control, although its advocates were influenced by different motives. In 1925, the NUSEC incorporated birth control as part of its regular list of resolutions. For Eleanor Rathbone and her followers, birth control was considered as an essential aspect of the welfare feminism programme as it would ease the woman's burden within the family. More radical feminists such as Naomi Mitchison and Margaret Cole viewed birth control as a means of liberating the expression of women's sexuality. It was certainly the case that birth control was a major contributory factor behind the fall in the birth rate during the inter-war years as the chart below illustrates.[16]

Birth Rates per 1000 pop.

	England & Wales	Scotland
1901–05	28.2	29.2
1906–10	26.3	27.6
1911–15	23.6	25.4
1916–20	20.0	22.8
1921–25	19.9	23.0
1926–30	16.7	20.0
1931–35	15.0	18.2
1936–40	14.7	17.6

Correlated with the fall in the birth rate was a reduction in the average size of families, with those numbering three or more children declining and those with one to two increasing. The implications for women were that some of the hardships of childbearing were alleviated after 1918, although the benefits were felt more directly by middle-class rather than working-class women.

5 Conclusion

In assessing the economic and social progress of women during the inter-war years, it would appear that many of the wartime developments concerning women had proven transitory. National economic

> **KEY ISSUE** To what extent did women's lives improve after the First World War?

problems undermined women's economic independence, forcing women to concede many of their wartime gains. In addition, jobs for women were perceived to be inconsequential compared to the importance of reinstating men in peacetime jobs. As a result, female employment was relegated to a level where women no longer challenged men, either in relation to skills, status or pay. Those who did so were the exception. However, the policy of prioritising jobs for men was endorsed by many of the women who had worked during the war on the grounds that men were the primary breadwinners. So although the government clearly adhered to policies which encouraged a return to domesticity, these ideas matched many women's expectations that work had been but a temporary interruption to their lives.

As the evidence on women's employment illustrates, the economic trends after 1918 suggest that women's progress was checked by a combination of carefully construed policies, economic constraints and an ideology which promoted domesticity. However, women's achievements should not be dismissed. The opening up of professional careers to women may have been slow, but at least women had the opportunity to challenge male attitudes regarding their capabilities as professionals. These were key developments in helping to shape future impressions of women's role in society. The significance of increased employment in light industry is more questionable. In one respect it gave women the chance to earn independent income but, at the same time, women's skills were devalued by the nature of the work. It was also clear that, despite the activities of the feminist movement, an insufficient number of women thought to question their secondary status in the labour market. In many respects, therefore, there was both change and continuity in the nature of women's economic role in society after 1918.

The other key issue to evaluate is whether the First World War had acted as an agent of social change for women. Also, to what extent were women themselves instrumental in sustaining the progress gained both before and during the war? There is certainly a strong case for arguing that the war, combined with the franchise in 1918, had given women even greater confidence to persist with various campaigns. As the prospect of political equality appeared more feasible, so the need for equal rights in other areas became even more compelling. Despite the divisions within feminism, which weakened the impact of the women's movement, the motivation to campaign for women's rights was very strong. The legislative reforms of the 1920s especially are testament to the dedicated work undertaken by numerous women's organisations.

So despite those achievements, we are still faced with the dilemma that so many women appeared after 1918 to acquiesce in a policy of domesticity. As arguments about the value of family allowances prevailed, it would seem that women were content to forgo much of the independence which they had acquired during the war. But were women's lives worse off as a result? One key change was the increasingly open discussion about women's sexuality, their relationship within a marriage, combined with the growing opportunity to determine the size of their family. This must be regarded as of singular importance for women's self-esteem in that women could begin to reverse the perception that they were always socially dependent on men. Although many women found themselves confined to the home again, within that home they were beginning to acquire a greater degree of autonomy. Likewise, as entertainments such as the cinema and dance halls gained in popularity and people's mobility increased with the use of the motor car, so women had the opportunity to escape from the domestic routine. These changes in social behaviour clearly reflected wartime developments when women had first experienced independence on a large scale. Thus the inter-war years can be interpreted as a time of mixed experiences for women. For many middle and upper-class women, the progress was perceptible and significant. For working-class women, change was more measured.

References

1 Cheryl Law, *Suffrage and Power: the Women's Movement 1918–1928* (I.B.Taurus, 1997), p. 68.
2 Deidre Beddoes, *Back to Home and Duty* (Pandora, 1989), p. 49.
3 Quoted in Harold Smith, ed., *Feminism in the Twentieth Century* (Edward Elgar Publishing Ltd., 1990), p. 52.
4 Women's Freedom League, *16th Annual Conference*, 28 April 1923 (Box 57, GB/106/2/WFL6/2/13), p. 2.
5 A.H. Halsey, ed., *British Social Trends Since 1900* (Macmillan, 1988), p. 172.
6 Elizabeth Roberts, *Women's Work, 1840–1940* (Cambridge University Press, 1988), p. 30.
7 Martin Pugh, *Women and the Women's Movement in Britain 1914–1959* (Macmillan, 1992), p. 94.
8 Jennifer Hart, *Ask Me No More* (Peter Haliban, 1998), p. 82.
9 Betty D. Vernon, *Ellen Wilkinson 1891–1947* (Croom Helm, 1982), p. 96.
10 Quoted in Jane Lewis, *Women in England 1870–1950: Sexual Divisions and Social Change* (Wheatsheaf Books Ltd., 1984), p. 35.
11 Carol Dyhouse, *Feminism and the Family in England 1880–1939* (Blackwell, 1989), p. 67.
12 Eleanor Rathbone, *The Disinherited Family* (Edward Arnold and Co., 1924), p. 262.
13 *The Times*, 11 February, 1929, p. 8.
14 Winifred Holtby, *Women* (John Lane The Bodley Head, 1939), p. 148.
15 Marie Stopes, *Married Love* (Victor Gollancz, 1995), p. 43.
16 Halsey, ed., *British Social Trends*, p. 40.

Summary Diagram
Economic and Social Change, 1918–39

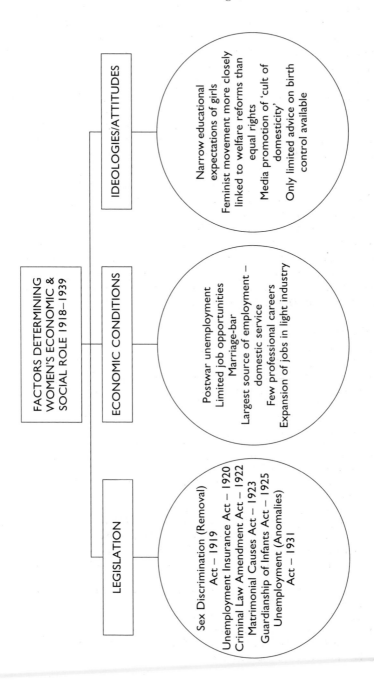

FACTORS DETERMINING WOMEN'S ECONOMIC & SOCIAL ROLE 1918–1939

IDEOLOGIES/ATTITUDES

Narrow educational expectations of girls
Feminist movement more closely linked to welfare reforms than equal rights
Media promotion of 'cult of domesticity'
Only limited advice on birth control available

ECONOMIC CONDITIONS

Postwar unemployment
Limited job opportunities
Marriage-bar
Largest source of employment – domestic service
Few professional careers
Expansion of jobs in light industry

LEGISLATION

Sex Discrimination (Removal) Act – 1919
Unemployment Insurance Act – 1920
Criminal Law Amendment Act – 1922
Matrimonial Causes Act – 1923
Guardianship of Infants Act – 1925
Unemployment (Anomalies) Act – 1931

Having read through the chapter, you should have gained a reasonable understanding of the different factors which affected the nature of women's role in society between the wars. You now need to think more carefully about how and why these developments occurred. You also need to appreciate the issue of change and continuity, the extent to which women's social and economic circumstances improved, remained the same, or reverted to pre-war conditions.

In examining the question of how and why various developments occurred, you can adopt a number of different approaches. For each of the key issues in the chapter, use the sub-heading 'What happened' and write down brief bullet points. Then put the heading 'Why?'. For example, on the question of women's employment you should evaluate the significance of the First World War, the immediate post-war economic crisis, government policies and women's attitudes towards the question of employment. Do this for all the main sections of the chapter.

The other approach is to establish links between different parts of the chapter. For example, it is important to evaluate the response of the feminist movement to all the issues concerning women after 1918. Make headings of those issues, such as family allowances, employment, equal pay, birth control, and note down the views of both the 'new' and 'equality' feminists. Make sure you can explain why they held these views. Other thematic analysis could focus on the effects of legislation, or society's views of women.

Finally, you need to reach some conclusion regarding the extent to which conditions changed for women between the wars. Go back over the notes you have already made, and then try to write two to three succinct paragraphs, giving your opinions and backing those ideas with facts.

Answering structured and essay questions on Chapter 4

Look at the following questions:

1. Women's Economic Role in the Inter-War Years

a) What were the reasons for the increase in women's unemployment at the end of the First World War? (*5 marks*)
b) To what extent did the pattern of employment change after 1918? (*10 marks*)
c) How influential were the attitudes of both men and women in determining the nature of women's work after 1918? (*15 marks*)

Hints and advice: Questions 1a) and 1b) are intended as a means of helping you to check your understanding of a key section of this chapter. It will be helpful to make a concise list of reasons for 1a) before placing them in some order of priority. Good answers will explain the interaction of a range of causal factors. 1b) will require you to incorporate some of the points you learnt in Chapter 2 on women's employment so that you can judge the extent to which employment patterns changed. 1c) is similar to the questions set in Chapter 3 in that your ideas have to reflect levels of importance. Identify the key attributes of male/female attitudes and then ask how far these attitudes explain the nature of women's work. For example, what are the links between men considering that they were the 'breadwinners' and women doing only unskilled work? Use each paragraph to analyse a main point of your argument and make sure that you include your evaluation of that point. Don't forget that you also need to demonstrate some understanding that other factors also influenced the type of work that women undertook in the inter-war years.

Now consider the following essay questions:

2. How far was the government responsible for the 'domestication' of women after 1918?
3. 'Feminism was in a state of decline after 1918'. Discuss
4. To what extent did the First World War act as a watershed in women's lives?

Whilst Questions 2 and 3 are based purely on Chapter 4, Question 4 is a much broader question which incorporates material you have read in Chapters 1, 2 and 3 as well. The issue of whether the First World War acted as a watershed in women's lives was raised in Chapter 1 and should be addressed before you move on to the next chapters in the book. You will want to re-evaluate this question at the end of the book, but at this stage you should consider carefully the overall implications of the war in relation to women's role in society. You can divide your essay into three main sections – political, social and economic – but remember that you will only be able to evaluate change in fairly broad terms. Select relevant evidence, but deploy this alongside a discussion which looks at both immediate and more long-term change.

Source-based questions on Chapter 4

1. Women and the Family, 1918–39
Study the two illustrations on pages 68 and 70 and read the extracts by Winifred Holtby and Marie Stopes on page 69.

a) What does Winifred Holtby mean by the phrase 'good wives and mothers' (line 11)? (*3 marks*)
b) What do the illustration on page 70 and the extract by Marie Stopes reveal about changing attitudes amongst women towards sexual relationships? (*4 marks*)

c) How useful is the illustration on page 68 as an example of women's interests in the 1930s? (*5 marks*)

d) Look at all four sources. To what extent do these sources reflect the dilemmas which women faced regarding their roles both within and without the family between 1918 and 1939? (*8 marks*)

Hints and advice: Question 1a) tests your comprehension of the source and in particular the reference to 'good wives and mothers'. A good answer will recognise that 'good wives and mothers' had both positive and negative attributes. With Question 1b) it is important to appreciate the historical context in which both sources were produced. The sources should act as a prompt with which you can then discuss the nature of changing attitudes and perhaps women's likely reactions to the sources. Question 1c) requires you to evaluate the source not only as an example of women's interests in the 1930s but also the utility of the source in its own right. What are its strengths and limitations as a source? Your own knowledge should help you to draw some conclusions about its utility. Finally, Question 1d) is intended to encourage further analysis of the dilemmas women faced regarding their status within and without the family. Each source should give some insights, although again your own knowledge should provide some criteria against which you can test the extent to which the sources are really helpful.

5 The Second World War, 1939–45

POINTS TO CONSIDER

The main issue to consider whilst reading this chapter is whether the Second World War acted as a further watershed in changing the nature of women's roles in society. Many developments will be similar to those which occurred during the First World War, but you should endeavour to identify changes such as new economic opportunities, greater social freedoms and more political involvement in government which were possibly more extensive. By the end of the chapter you should have some sense of the relative importance of these changes for women's future position within British society.

KEY DATES

1939	**3 Sept**	Britain declared war on Germany.
1940	**Feb**	Backbench women MPs formed the Woman Power Committee.
	Mar	Ernest Bevin set up Women's Consultative Committee.
	10 May	Neville Chamberlain resigned; Winston Churchill became Prime Minister.
1941	**Mar**	First Womanpower Debate.
	Mar	The Registration of Employment Order.
	Dec	The National Service (No.2) Act.
1942	**Jan**	All women aged 20–21 called up.
	Feb	The Employment of Women (Control of Engagement) Order.
	Mar	Second Womanpower Debate.
	Dec	Publication of Beveridge Report.
1943	**Apr**	Equal Compensation for war injuries.
1944	**Aug**	Butler Education Act passed.

1 Introduction

> **KEY ISSUES** What were the similarities and differences between the First and Second World Wars concerning opportunities for women? How significant were those developments?

As with the First World War, the Second World War prompted important changes in women's employment patterns, resulting in significant increases in the percentage of women working. Jobs in light industry largely declined to be gradually replaced by widening opportunities in heavy industry, especially munitions, as well as a range of associated manufacturing industries. Increasingly, gaps in the labour market were filled by women, whether in white-collar jobs, the professions or on the land. War also had a major impact on women's social lives in the sense that women's commitments to their families had to be managed alongside the need to work outside the home. The strains and stresses on private lives were just as acute.

There were, however, a number of important differences relating to the Second World War which suggest that women were affected on a far greater scale than was the case in 1914. First, Britain was the only participating country in the Second World War to conscript women into either what were designated as essential industries or the armed services. Whether in paid employment or attached to the voluntary services, women played a more prominent role in the war effort than before. Women were in the frontline on an unprecedented scale.

Second, the war of 1939 was much more global, requiring a massive support system for the military. In addition, it caused major civilian disruption throughout Great Britain. Thus women were central to the daily routines of coping with the effects of bombing as well as endeavouring to preserve family life. Yet, with so many women working away from home, conventional patterns of behaviour were easily undermined as women experienced greater social freedoms. The fact that few women could escape involvement in the war meant that the opportunities to change the direction of their lives, to experience new roles, were far more widespread.

The final important difference regarding the Second World War was that, with political emancipation in 1918 and 1928, women were now in Parliament. Unlike 1914–18, women MPs could participate in debates about the war, they could hope to influence government policies. The extent to which they were successful will be discussed in Section 4, but it is important to recognise here that with such extensive involvement of women in the war effort, it was vital that their interests were represented and protected in Parliament.

Historians still disagree as to whether the war instigated fundamental changes for women or not. It is this question, therefore, of the extent to which the war acted as a watershed for women's role in society which will form the underlying analysis of this chapter.

2 Women's Role in the National Economy

> **KEY ISSUE** What contribution did women make to Britain's economy during the Second World War?

a) The Immediate Economic Consequences of War

As with the First World War, the government was slow to maximise the potential economic value of women's labour when war broke out in

September 1939. In particular, the government failed to compensate for the effects on manpower of calling up all men aged 18 to 41 into the armed forces, unless they worked in essential 'reserved' occupations. This inaction was compounded by the fact that, during this period of the 'Phoney War', over a million men remained unemployed. Consequently, there was little inclination to utilise the large numbers of women who were volunteering to work in industrial and non-industrial sectors as well as the voluntary services. In August 1939 alone, 30,000 women had volunteered to join the Women's Land Army, but once their training was completed, thousands were directed back to the Labour Exchanges. The Auxiliary Territorial Service (ATS) – the women's section of the army – had begun large-scale recruiting in Spring 1939, but was likewise unable to cope efficiently, lacking sufficient uniforms and accommodation for the new recruits. Two months after the commencement of the war the Ministry of Information told women that unless they were very well qualified, they should either stay in their current jobs or be at home.

Similar confusion applied to women's employment in industry. The contraction of consumer and light industries was not matched by a corresponding expansion of opportunities for women in war production. Women who had worked in light industries, such as textiles, hosiery and glove making now faced redundancy as non-essential productions were reduced. In textiles alone, some 20,000 women lost their jobs. But opportunities in wartime production failed to materialise. The Women's Employment Federation was overwhelmed by women seeking jobs in 1939, especially from women with good educational qualifications, but less than half of the 6,872 who registered were found jobs.[1] Whereas male unemployment declined after 1939, that of women rose and did not drop below pre-war levels until February 1941. The problem was that, after 1918, employers had encouraged the employment of women in lighter, repetitive, less-skilled jobs, or low grade clerical work. Any erosion of that policy would undermine men's skilled status.

b) The Government Response – Direction and Conscription

Several factors compelled the government to re-evaluate its laissez-faire approach to women's employment. The loss of Britain's European allies to Nazi occupation had serious implications, leaving Britain isolated in the defence against Germany. Britain's industry was ill-prepared to guarantee the supplies needed for the army, air-force and navy. Despite having retained all appropriate manpower in essential industries, it was clear that output was totally inadequate.

Until 1941, the government relied on a voluntary system of involvement in war work. A range of options were open to women: enrolment in one or other of the women's sections of the Armed Forces – the ATS, the Women's Auxiliary Air Force (WAAF), the Women's Royal

Naval Service (WRENS); nursing; working in the Women's Land Army; joining Civil Defence units or undertaking voluntary work with organisations such as the Women's Voluntary Service (WVS). As for jobs in industry, there was no official system of registering women for work, so although women were available for employment they were not directed to areas of greatest need. Nonetheless, by late 1940 the Manpower Requirements Committee estimated that an additional two million women would be needed in industry.

The first official directions were made in March 1941 when Bevin introduced the Registration of Employment Order (see the table opposite). However, the government's handling of the campaign caused considerable confusion. Officials lacked the answers to key questions regarding pay, hours, childcare support for mothers, and whether women would have to work away from home. In addition, the notion that the scheme was calling for volunteers was undermined when it looked as if all women aged 20 and 21 would be compulsorily registered. As the *Daily Sketch*, usually a supporter of the government, alleged in an editorial on 20 March 1941,

 ı It is high time for Mr Ernest Bevin to tell the country precisely what he does mean by his proposals for the conscription of women ... At the present moment no woman in Great Britain knows *where she stands and the husbands, brothers and sons of all our women are in the same state of*
 5 *uncertainty.*[2]

Government hopes that more efficient management of a voluntary registration system would result in adequate supplies of labour were ill-founded. By August 1941, of the two million women who had been registered, only 500,000 had been interviewed and a mere 87,000 had gone to work either in munitions or the Women's Auxiliary Services.[3] By the end of 1941, it was decided that clearer direction was needed, namely that of conscription. A number of acts were introduced (see the table opposite) which gradually tightened the government's control over female employment. In implementing this legislation, Britain became the only country to introduce compulsion for women but it had become necessary in order to overcome continuing labour shortages. Those who refused direction were liable to a fine of five pounds a day or imprisonment. In January 1942 Constance Bolan became the first woman to be convicted and imprisoned for a month for refusing to do hospital work.

Somewhat reluctantly, the government was also compelled to extend the call-up to women with domestic responsibilities. Mobile recruiting vans toured the country as part of the campaign to persuade such women, including mothers, to undertake part-time work. Between January 1942 and June 1944, the number of part-time female employees increased from 380,000 to 900,000, whilst registration was further increased to include all women up to the age of 50. The result of this mobilisation meant that thousands of British women were now fully involved in all aspects of wartime production.

The Introduction of Compulsion for Women's Employment

March 1941 The Registration of Employment Order
This required women aged 19–40 to register at their local Employment Exchange where they could be directed towards useful war work, with the threat of compulsion if they refused.

December 1941 The National Service (No.2) Act
Single women aged 20–30 were liable for service either in the Women's Auxiliary Services or for employment in the munitions industries. A category of 'mobile' women was introduced whereby single women who had no household responsibilities could be moved out of their home area to one where there was an urgent demand for labour. Another category, 'Household R', exempted women, single or married, who were considered to have domestic responsibilities, however limited, whilst those with children under the age of 14 were also excluded.

January 1942
The first call up to all women aged 20–21 was issued.

February 1942 The Employment of Women (Control of Engagement) Order
All women aged 20–30 had to be employed through Employment Exchanges.

January 1943
The upper age limit was extended to 40 whilst many housewives who had previously been exempt were now directed into part-time work.

c) Women's Contributions to the War Effort

By 1943 over 443,000 women had joined the auxiliary branches of the Armed Forces – the ATS, WAAF and WRNS. Within each organisation recruits provided essential back-up support ranging from unskilled jobs such as waitressing in a sergeants' mess to more skilled jobs, such as maintaining radar operations, manning air barrage balloons, working as flight mechanics or engineers or even conducting reconnaissance photography. Although women were not permitted to be active soldiers because soldiering was seen as exclusively 'men's work', their involvement proved vital in ensuring the success of military operations.

Thousands of women were also recruited into the Women's Land Army, which was under civilian rather than military control. New recruits would enrol to train at colleges or carefully selected farms before being allocated to a specific farm. Some lodged in hostels from where they were taken in gangs to work, while others were billeted with individual farmers. For many town girls who had barely seen a

green field in their lives, the work could be gruelling – digging pota-
toes, milking cows, operating tractors, carting farm muck, drilling, as
well as enduring long hours during busy times like harvesting.

The other major source of employment for women was in 'essential
industries' with the result that whereas in 1939 women made up 14 per
cent of this workforce, by 1943 this figure had risen to 33 per cent. Women
who had previously been employed as shopkeepers, waitresses, clerical
workers and in low skilled factory work were transferred to engineering,
chemicals, shipbuilding, transport which all concentrated on output for
the war effort. They were also joined by thousands of young women, often
young middle-class girls, who had no previous experience of work. Hours
were long, often involving shifts from 8 a.m. to midnight, seven days a
week. The most dangerous work occurred in the Royal Ordnance
Factories where munitions were produced. Here work ranged from the
monotonous filling of shells, or drilling holes in brass plates, to making
shell cases, welding and riveting metal. In other factories, women learnt
to repair aircraft such as the Spitfires, patching up holes in the wings.

Women made similar advances in the non-industrial sectors. In
banks, some women were promoted from typical menial clerical work
to dealing with customers at the counters. The Post Office, always a
bastion of male influence, reluctantly permitted women to deliver the
post, whilst in education and the Civil Service thousands of women
who had relinquished their positions when they got married now
returned to their professional careers. However, in the Civil Service it
was invariably the case that well-qualified women were kept on lower
rates of pay because they were deemed to be only temporary staff.

Further opportunities arose for women within the voluntary sector,
which undertook the huge task of civil defence. By 1942 there were
over 19,000 full-time workers in civil defence, driving ambulances,
acting as Air Raid Protection Wardens, running first aid posts and shel-
ters, undertaking fire-guard duties and acting as emergency messen-
gers. In 1943 the government ordered that Voluntary Civil Defence
Work become compulsory even if women were working all day.

Another key organisation was the Women's Voluntary Service
(WVS) whose members became essential co-ordinators of civilian welfare. The government had failed to prepare adequately for the severe
disruption caused by the evacuation of women and children at the
beginning of the war, and the chaos which ensued during the relentless bombing raids. In towns and cities across Britain, refugees made
homeless by bombing came to rely on the WVS for mobile canteens
and laundries, feeding and rest centres, temporary billeting, clothing
exchanges and help in tracing missing relatives. The country lacked
an official welfare system that could provide comprehensive care for
the many displaced people. Instead, it was female volunteers who
initiated and managed a vital component of the war effort.

Additional volunteer help came from the Women's Institute (WI)
which, out of deference to its Quaker members, restricted its activities

to a non-militant nature. Hence tasks such as saving and preserving tons of summer fruits were undertaken; in 1942 alone, 1,764 tons of preserves were produced by the WI at preservation centres across the country as can be seen in the illustration (on page 84) of women from the Brimpton Women's Institute. Of equal value was the assistance given by WIs with the problems arising from evacuation, organising collection of clothes, household essentials and helping families to adjust to the unfamiliar pattern of rural life.

Women's contributions were widely recognised as being indispensable in resisting defeat by Germany, a fact which was acknowledged by Churchill at the National Conference of Women in 1943:

1 This war effort could not have been achieved if the women had not marched forward in millions and undertaken all kinds of tasks and work for which any other generation but our own ... would have considered them unfitted: work in the fields, heavy work in the foundries and in the
5 shops, very refined work on radio and precision instruments, work in the hospitals, responsible clerical work of all kinds, work throughout the munitions factories, work in the mixed batteries.[4]

3 The Change in Gender Roles

> **KEY ISSUES** To what extent did the war successfully erode traditional gender roles? How did women's personal perceptions of their role in society change and was this merely a short-term development?

In order to understand the extent to which women's roles were affected, several factors need to be evaluated: the effect of new employment opportunities, the impact of greater social freedoms on women and the extent to which further social and economic emancipation was welcomed or discouraged by both men and women.

a) The Significance of Shifting Patterns of Employment

Historians have developed a number of different interpretations as to whether gender barriers were reinforced or broken down as a result of new employment opportunities for women. Arthur Marwick, in 1974, advocated the view that war prompted what he termed as 'an irreversible trend'[5] in the employment of married women, as well as creating greater social and economic freedoms overall. In contrast, Penny Summerfield has argued that whilst war did not fully emancipate women, it did challenge traditional gender divisions, causing women to develop wider expectations for themselves after 1945. Lucy Noakes has claimed that although many gender barriers were broken, feminine and masculine distinctions remained, ensuring that women's secondary role endured. Harold L. Smith has offered the

Preparing Fruit for Jam Making

most dismissive viewpoint of the effect of the war in that he perceived little in terms of immediate change and only minimal, long-term change for women.

Differing interpretations of statistics illustrate how difficult it is to gain a consensus. Estimates by the Ministry of Labour in 1941 calculated that over 80 per cent of all single women aged 14-59, 41 per cent of all wives and widows and 13 per cent of all mothers with children under 14 were in work or in uniform with the auxiliary forces.[6] These apparent trends were also observed by Penny Summerfield, who noted that the proportion of married women working had gone up from a pre-war level of 16 per cent in 1931 to 43 per cent by 1943. Overall, the percentage of women aged 35-59 who worked increased to 42 per cent of the total female workforce by 1943, whereas those aged 25 and under decreased from a pre-war level of 41 per cent to 27 per cent. Summerfield concluded that 'there was a substantially increased proportion of working wives during the war' which was 'consistent with the undisputed war-time rise in the proportion of women workers who were married, and the shift to an older age profile of women workers'.[7] This contrasted with inter-war attitudes which had discouraged married women from working (see page 57).

The evidence which suggests that a higher proportion of women, and especially older women, worked during the war would seem quite conclusive. Harold L. Smith, however, has focused on the fact that for large numbers of women, wartime employment was not a new experience. According to a Wartime Social Survey conducted in 1943, only 28 per cent claimed not to have worked before the war, whilst only 25 per cent anticipated that they would want to work after the war was over. Smith's main thesis is that changes in employment patterns had already commenced before the war and that only a small percentage change can be attributed to the war itself. Smith also points to the fact that despite the number of women employed full-time in industry, the armed forces and civil defence (7,250,000 in 1943), they were outnumbered by women who remained full-time housewives (8,770,000).[8] Clearly the difference in emphasis amongst historians has resulted in a measure of disagreement.

The extent to which women's work remained segregated during wartime is also debatable. Despite statistics which show that women undertook work of a 'masculine' nature, skilled jobs were often split up into unskilled tasks. As with the First World War, this policy of dilution provided the justification for lower rates of pay. When the principle of equal pay for equal work was demanded, resistance – based largely on male fears that overall rates of pay would be lowered – prevailed. Thus there was the concept of 'women's pay' and 'women's work', both convenient labels by which to explain differences in pay. In 1945 women earned on average 52 per cent of men's wages.

The overall impact of the war on women's employment can ultimately only be truly evaluated when post-war trends in employment are assessed. As Lucy Noakes has identified, 37 per cent of all women employed in 1943 worked in the munitions industry, a form of employment that was largely exclusive to wartime.[9] This was inevitably a temporary change which would result in large numbers being dismissed at the end of the war. However, there is evidence that the overall pattern of employment did undergo permanent developments. Although the percentage of women working within various industries dropped with the resumption of peace, in general the numbers were approximately double the 1939 figures.

	1939	1943	1959
Engineering	10	34	21
Metal & Manufacturing	6	22	12
Transport	5	20	13
White-collar workers	17	46	38

Women as a Percentage of the Workforce[10]

Most significantly, the increase in more married women working was sustained in peacetime. Initially numbers declined to 40 per cent in 1947 as many women were anxious to devote more time to their families, but by 1959 this figure had increased to 59 per cent. It seems that the experience of working during the war had set in motion a trend which was not wholly negated by the return to peace in 1945.

b) Women's Response to New Employment Opportunities

The contention that war did accelerate or promote a breakdown in traditional gender roles is further substantiated when the issue of women's attitudes is examined. Work opened up new horizons for women although it was also the source of considerable stress. Consequently, women's reactions to work varied considerably according to their experiences.

One valuable source of contemporary opinion is provided by a project known as the Mass Observation survey, conducted between 1937 and 1949, which involved both a series of observations undertaken by volunteers and personal diaries kept by members of the public. One report made by Diana Brinton Lee revealed the mixed response of many factory workers to their work. She admitted that the war had changed the pre-war tendency for female labour to be recruited only on a short-term basis from young unmarried women. The most significant change focused on older women, for whom part-time work had given a new interest in life.

1 When you get up in the morning you feel you go out with something in your bag, and something coming in at the end of the week, and it's nice. It's a taste of independence, and you feel a lot happier for it. ... I have everything to do at home, and so all I want is to get on to part-time. It's
5 just what you can imagine nicely when you are middle-age.[11]

This evidence was supported by other surveys which suggested that older married women were more inclined to remain in employment after the war. The Wartime Social Survey, for example, found that 59 per cent of part-time female workers wanted to continue with work once the war was over. Although many of these married women had worked before, for them the extra money plus the companionship of work, and the fact that they were less house-bound, were all strong incentives to resist a return to a purely domestic life.

For thousands of young women, many of whom had been domestic servants, factory work clearly offered better pay, companionship and independence, as well as greater social freedom to go to dances and the cinema. On the other hand, there was little job satisfaction in the monotonous daily tasks of the factory workshop and many felt little empathy with the object of their work – the war effort. Thus amongst younger women war work was generally perceived as a temporary interruption before settling down to get married.

Of course when we get married I shan't want to work; I shall want to stay at home and have some children. You can't look on anything you do during the war as what you really mean to do; it's just filling in time till you can live your own life again.[12]

Women who worked for the armed forces, civil defence or the Land Army often experienced a higher level of job satisfaction. The work had the potential to be more challenging and adventurous; for middle and upper-class girls the work gave them their first chance of leaving home. As one member of the Women's Land Army noted,

> The Land Army work was hard, dangerous and dirty, but while the men were fighting we were doing what we could. Most of us felt like that. War work certainly made many young women independent for the first time. Suddenly you could earn your own money and spend it how you
> 5 wished. We had more freedom. We could go to the pictures by ourselves, go to dances.[13]

It would appear, therefore, that for many women work resulted in greater self-confidence. Greater independence also forced many women to grow up and to see beyond the narrow confines of life at home. As one girl commented, at the end of the war, 'Going to live at home again was pretty grim, because Dad was always very strict. It was like having your wings clipped. I spent a lot of time round at a girl friend's'.[14] For other women, however, wartime employment did little to change traditional attitudes regarding their personal lives.

c) Marriage, Family and Sexual Relationships

The war not only helped to expose women to new economic opportunities, it also created an environment in which attitudes towards marriage and the family were changing. As with the First World War, women again assumed authority for managing households, but with such extensive mobilisation of women into war work the upheaval to family life was far more dramatic. Journeys to work could take up as much as three hours per day, particularly when Royal Ordnance Factories were located far away from towns. Normal daily routines were totally disrupted with women combining nightshift work with daily tasks of washing, cooking, queuing for rations, cleaning, and getting children to school or nursery. Absenteeism amongst married women was twice as high as that of men because no provisions were made to permit women time off to manage their domestic responsibilities. There were also the problems of 'making do', of having to deal with wartime economies resulting from widespread rationing. The strain of coping was further aggravated by the lack of nurseries; despite the fact that by 1944 there were about 1,500 wartime day nurseries compared with only 14 in October 1940, demand still exceeded supply, and only one quarter of all children under the age of five of women war workers were in nurseries.

The effects of such responsibilities were considerable. Many women longed for peace and the chance to resume normal married life. For others war imposed extensive strains on their marriages as women found themselves either working away from home or struggling with family life on their own. Loneliness, combined with a strong desire to have a 'good time', helped to break down normal patterns of social behaviour. There was a marked increase in infidelity amongst married couples, whilst single people of both sexes were more inclined to embark on intense friendships, conscious that the realities of war could curtail a relationship at any time. Yet the moral rebuke against women who transgressed over acceptable lines of behaviour was still very strong. Women in the armed forces, for example, knew that to walk home alone from a dance at night would be inviting trouble and were anxious to avoid any allegations of promiscuity. The pressures, however, to be more sexually available were considerable, especially when so many servicemen and American GIs were based in Britain.

Critics point to the increased rate of illegitimacy which rose from 4.4 per cent of all live births in 1939 to 9.1 per cent in 1945 as evidence that there was a decline of morals during wartime. However, such an increase was more probably attributable to the exceptional circumstances arising from the strains of life in wartime. Prior to the war, if women got pregnant they would endeavour to avoid the stigma of an illegitimate birth by getting married before the birth of the child. Such a solution was more difficult during the war when servicemen only had limited leave. Hence fewer expectant mothers were able to marry in order to legitimise a birth. Yet although women knew they would be reproached for such misdemeanours, society was generally more tolerant of illegitimacy than it had been before 1939.

As women experienced greater freedoms, so divorce rates rose, most notably at the end of the war when couples had to face up to whether they could resume a relationship disrupted by long separation, changing gender roles and the consequent strain on the marriage. In 1946, 58 per cent of the petitions for divorce were filed by husbands, and of those, 75 per cent were for adultery. Amongst women there was a steady increase in those citing cruelty as grounds for divorce.

The resumption of peace in 1945 held important implications for women's status within the family. Undoubtedly many welcomed the chance to resume normal relations with their husbands. Most men and women assumed that men were still the breadwinners, but many women now looked for a greater share of responsibilities within the family. The notion that women were the dependent partner was finally being challenged, although not yet defeated, by the view that women were entitled to greater domestic equality.

d) Male Attitudes

Another contributory factor that helped to determine the extent to which the emancipation experienced by women during the war was temporary or permanent was the reaction of men to women's changing circumstances. As Edith Summerskill commented in her autobiography, it was difficult to change male opinions:

The average man's conception of a woman's capabilities is formed by his experiences in his own home where his wife and his daughters set a pattern of behaviour; consequently war calls for a tremendous readjustment of preconceived ideas. For a woman to work outside the home
5 disturbs some men. They privately believe perhaps that their wives may be subjected to unwelcome advances; consequently there is a conflict between personal desires and the needs of the country.[15]

The government was especially conscious of the level of anxiety displayed by men in the armed forces towards the number of women with domestic responsibilities going out to work. Somehow the government had to resolve the dilemma of wanting to encourage women to do their duty to the country, whilst not undermining their roles as housewives and mothers. Thus propaganda aimed at women was carefully designed to convey key images of women's contribution to the war effort. Cheerful pictures of Land Girls working in the fields, glowing posters exhorting women to join one of the armed services (as seen in the poster on page 90), all suggested that women were both vital to the nation's defence and willing participants in that campaign. Yet, underlying this publicity was a very strong emphasis on the importance of women retaining their femininity. As the recruitment poster for the WAAF reveals, women could still be glamorous even when in uniform. Moreover, their role was clearly to assist the men, rather than to work in an equal capacity.

Women were portrayed as being the pivotal line of defence on the Home Front. Government propaganda via the press and radio continually plied women with advice on how to provide healthy, nourishing meals, as well as giving tips on domestic economy. Likewise, regular guidance on childcare reminded women of their duty to rear healthy children. But women were also encouraged not to let the struggle of running a home on limited resources undermine their feminine qualities. Hints on how to enhance personal appearances, despite wartime shortages of clothes and cosmetics, proliferated in women's magazines. Women's personal morale had to be sustained despite the gloom of wartime austerity.

The emphasis on promoting women's femininity and preserving distinct gender roles was also evident in educational lectures organised by the Army Bureau for Current Affairs for men and women serving in the Armed Forces. These lectures were carefully constructed, first to allay men's concerns about women's participation in the war effort, and secondly to ensure that men and women maintained different expectations of their respective roles in society. In one lecture entitled 'Woman's Place', the author attacked the notion that women should look for a career.

This slogan is usually repeated by upper-class feminists whose women-friends practise the more elegant professions – novelists, actresses, staff-managers and so on. It ignores the grim fact that most women who work are inevitably employed on rather wearisome jobs – such as fill-
5 ing bottles in factories ... Is there really anything more attractive to a

Serve in the WAAF with The Men Who Fly

woman in the prospect of a job of her own than in the prospect of a home of her own? ... Whatever else we look forward to after the war we must put first of all the principle that as many women as possible should marry and have babies.[16]

This policy towards women was further reflected in the Beveridge Report on the future of the welfare state which was published in 1942. It contained welcome proposals to introduce family allowances, the object of Eleanor Rathbone's persistent campaign, but it also included clear hints of what the government perceived to be the future role of women. For example it deterred married woman from resuming a career at a later stage because it would be difficult to regain her insurance rights. Beveridge commented:

the attitude of the housewife to gainful employment outside the home is not and should not be the same as the single woman ... housewives and mothers have vital work to do in ensuring the adequate continuance of the British race ... [17]

e) Conclusion

There are a number of indicators that suggest that women's social and economic emancipation during the war might have been more of a short-term phenomenon than a symptom of long-term change. Despite some women's determination to ensure that their status did not revert to pre-war conditions, the fairly explicit policies pursued by the government ensured that concepts of women's femininity and their duty to home and family were kept very much alive during the war. Without full endorsement from men in authority, and the thousands of men seeking peacetime employment in 1945, the continued emancipation of women might prove hard to sustain.

4 The Political Scene

> **KEY ISSUES** Did the war enhance or diminish the influence of women MPs within Parliament? In what areas of politics were they most effective?

In contrast to the inter-war years, when women MPs maintained primarily an allegiance to their own political party, between 1939 and 1945, a strong sense of cross-party cohesion developed. In addition, a number of women held posts within the government and so were directly involved in determining government policies. During the war, therefore, women in politics displayed a remarkable consensus in both articulating and seeking solutions to the concerns of women.

a) Pressure-Group Activity

One of the earlier signs that women MPs were prepared to act collectively came in spring 1940. A growing number of women were critical of Chamberlain's leadership, including Nancy Astor, Mavis Tate and Eleanor Rathbone. In a debate on 8 May 1940 Tate and Astor, along with 31 other government supporters, defied a three-line whip and so prompted the resignation of Neville Chamberlain. In the ensuing administration under Churchill, Florence Horsbrugh was retained as Junior Health Minister whilst Ellen Wilkinson became Parliamentary Secretary to the Minister of Pensions.

After the commencement of the war, women MPs soon focused their attention on the government's ineffective use of women's labour. Following representations from women's organisations, all the women backbenchers approached the Financial Secretary of the Treasury in February 1940 urging that women should be included more comprehensively in the war effort. The response was discouraging with the result that Nancy Astor established the Woman Power Committee consisting of all women backbenchers, which met fortnightly whilst Parliament was in session in order to examine women's issues. This committee developed into an effective lobbying group which regularly sought to influence government ideas. Its brief was to publicise problems affecting women and to make the government listen more attentively to women's views.

In March 1941, Ernest Bevin was finally persuaded to set up a Women's Consultative Committee, which included Edith Summerskill and Irene Ward, to act as an advisory body on women's labour. It was a decision which recognised that the problems of women's labour had to be managed more effectively than had hitherto been the case.

Further concerted pressure by women backbenchers on the government led to the first serious debate on the issue of womanpower in 1941. During the opening debate on 20 March 1941, Irene Ward emphasised women's determination to deploy their labour resources by whatever means necessary in order to help win the war. But, as became clear during the debate, such labour could only be properly utilised if adequate training facilities, decent working conditions and fair wages were provided, otherwise there would be little incentive to work. The debate articulated all the grievances which had prevailed since the start of the war. Above all, it drew attention to the fact that women were still being treated as second-class citizens at a time when they so clearly wished to be regarded as equal citizens. As Thelma Cazalet-Keir commented during the debate:

1 If we had 40 or 50 women Members of Parliament instead of the present small number, I doubt whether this Debate would have been necessary, because many of the things we are discussing today would either never have occurred or would have been automatically rectified
5 at a much earlier date ... [18]

Given that registration of women commenced in March 1941, to be followed by conscription in December 1941 (see page 81), this campaign to secure more effective management of woman-power was undoubtedly crucial in influencing government opinion. A second debate in March 1942 highlighted women's disappointment that, whilst they were struggling to support their country, they received very little help in managing their domestic responsibilities. Lack of nurseries was just one example of how the government ignored the realities of women's daily lives. Nursery provisions were never sufficient, but the government did recognise that further expansion was required. The prominent involvement of women MPs in the debate was a factor, therefore, in raising the profile of women's issues within Parliament.

Women MPs also intervened on the crucial question of equal compensation for injuries incurred as a result of the war. Women endured the same risks and were frequent casualties of bombing raids, but on average they received seven shillings (35p) a week less than men in compensation. Mavis Tate campaigned vigorously on this issue, including during the debate on the King's Speech on 25 November 1942. On this occasion, she forced the House to divide and vote on the question of equal compensation, gaining sufficient support to persuade the government to establish a Select Committee. This recommended the implementation of equal compensation, which came into force in April 1943.

Less successful were efforts to secure agreement on the long-standing issue of equal pay, the focus of campaigns throughout the inter-war years. After 1939, the huge influx of women onto the labour market highlighted the gross inequalities that women encountered in employment. With women MPs now acting as a more cohesive pressure group, there was for the first time a chance to force a reconsideration of rates of pay within the Commons. Edith Summerskill, through the auspices of the Women's Consultative Committee, endeavoured to obtain an agreement of equal pay for equal work when military conscription was introduced but failed to gain any concessions. The best chance of securing reform emerged when R.A. Butler's Education Bill was proposed in 1944. A clause to remove the marriage bar for teachers raised hopes that equal pay could also be included. Thelma Cazalet-Keir accordingly introduced an amendment which was passed by 117 to 116 votes. Unfortunately, the government's response destroyed any prospect of equal pay. Bevin threatened to resign if the amendment was sustained, whilst Churchill demanded a vote of confidence in his government on the issue. Government supporters, including Cazalet-Keir, abided by the three-line Whip and reversed the amendment rather than risk jeopardising the government's majority.

Despite this setback, the impact of the women MPs during the war was significant. They came closer to acting as a women's party than previously and they spoke collectively on a range of issues that concerned their sex rather than their political party. As a result, male MPs were compelled to treat women's issues more seriously. Women MPs also demonstrated that neither they nor their female constituents were content to let a male agenda dictate the management of the war. Their success in exerting pressure on the government was an important development in changing perceptions of women within political circles.

5 Conclusion

> **KEY ISSUE** How far had the Second World War been an agent of change for women?

Although there had been some progress regarding women's status during the inter-war years, a number of factors had kept their political, social and economic emancipation in check. But between 1939 and 1945 women had an opportunity to escape from the confines of domesticity and to demonstrate that they had the ability to serve the country in as valid a way as men. Indeed, their contribution to the defence of Britain, whether in industry, civil defence or the armed forces, was indispensable. It was also achieved in the face of unprecedented disruption to normal life. The tenacity of women to cope with major upheaval to daily routines and to throw such energy into the war effort was undoubtedly instrumental in helping to erode some traditional perceptions of women. But was this sufficient to ensure further emancipation for women?

In terms of their economic role in society, the outcome for women was mixed. As manpower resources diminished, so women proved themselves more than capable of doing men's work. But attitudes towards women in the workplace did not necessarily change in that both trade unions and employers viewed women's labour as a temporary solution to the shortages. Underlying problems remained, most notably that of lower wages and continued segregation of jobs which disadvantaged women. Only gradually did the government and employers appreciate the extent of women's grievances over issues such as inadequate childcare facilities, poor working conditions and a widespread lack of understanding of their domestic predicaments. Women naturally felt resentful that in comparison to their efforts they sometimes got little reward. It was not surprising that so many women wanted to return to a domestic life at the end of the war. Government policies towards women clearly had that objective in mind and gave women little encouragement to think differently.

However, not all women were ready to accept a return to a pre-war life-style. Whilst it would be impossible to generalise about the millions of women who had lived through the war, nevertheless attitudes amongst many women were more outward-looking, boosted by greater self-esteem and a confidence that they could exercise authority beyond the confines of the home. Women were more questioning of their status within relationships, less deferential to the traditional norms of behaviour. Even though marriage remained the main expectation for women, a goal that many desired after the stress of war, there was a stronger tendency for women to seek greater independence and more responsibilities within marriage.

One of the more long-term changes which occurred was the increase in numbers of married women working, especially on a part-time basis. This development, combined with changing attitudes about marriage, had important implications for their sense of independence and was a key factor in influencing the slow but steady emancipation of married women (see Chapter 6). However, given that society still expected women to be the main carers of children and the family, women had to become expert jugglers, managing work and family responsibilities in tandem.

As the country returned to peace in 1945, the future for women remained very uncertain. On the one hand, women's contribution to the war effort had had a significant impact on people's views. Moreover, women's opinions of themselves had progressed enormously. In many respects, therefore, war was an instigator of major changes in women's lives. But many underlying perceptions regarding women remained unchanged. Women were not considered as equal citizens either in politics, employment or within the family.

Furthermore, most women were not yet confident enough to challenge and change long-standing concepts of their role in society.

References

1 Penny Summerfield, *Women Workers in the Second World War* (Routledge, 1989), p. 32.
2 Cited in Dorothy Sheridan, ed., *Wartime Women* (Heinemann, 1990), pp. 133–4.
3 Summerfield, *Women Workers*, pp. 34–5.
4 Cited in John Costello, *Love, Sex and War: Changing Values, 1939–1945* (Collins, 1985), p. 214.
5 Arthur Marwick, *War and Social Change in the Twentieth Century* (Macmillan, 1974), p. 160.
6 Costello, *Love, Sex and War*, p. 197.
7 Penny Summerfield, 'Women, War and Social Change: Women in Britain in World War II', in Arthur Marwick, ed., *Total War and Social Change* (Macmillan, 1988), p. 101.
8 Harold L. Smith, 'The effect of the war on the status of women', in Harold L. Smith, ed., *War and Social Change: British Society in the Second World War* (Manchester University Press, 1986), p. 210.
9 Lucy Noakes, *War and the British Gender, Memory and National Identity* (I.B. Tauris, 1998), p. 20.
10 Summerfield, 'Women, War and Social Change', p. 98.
11 Angus Calder and Dorothy Sheridan, eds., *Speak For Yourself: A Mass Observation Anthology 1937–49* (Jonathan Cape, 1984), p. 179.
12 *Ibid.*, p. 181.
13 Cited in Pam Schweitzer, Lorraine Hilton, Jane Moss, eds., *What Did You Do in the War, Mum?* (Age Exchange Theatre Company, 1985), p. 4.
14 *Ibid.*, p. 17.
15 Edith Summerskill, *A Woman's World* (Heinemann, 1967), p. 75.
16 W.E. Williams, 'Woman's Place', *Current Affairs* (Army Bureau of Current Affairs), no.61, 29 January 1944, pp. 5, 8.
17 Cited in Smith, *War and Social Change*, p. 223.
18 *Parliamentary Debates*, Fifth Series, vol. 370, 20 March, 1941, cols. 346–347.

Summary Diagram
The Second World War, 1939–45

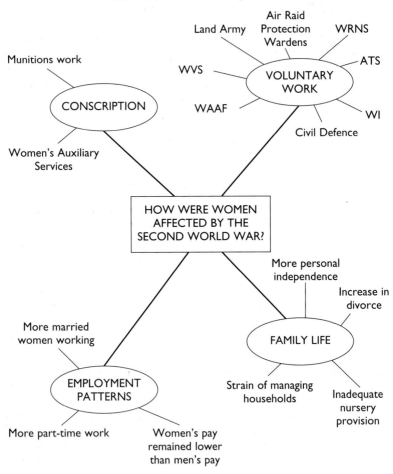

You should now have some sense of what were the changes affecting women that were either new or more extensive compared with their pre-war lives. Clarify your ideas on these points first, using the section headings in the chapter. Restrict yourself to main changes in employment, social behaviour, the family, and politics. This should assist you in identifying what was different about the Second World War in terms of the opportunities that opened up for women.

The next step is to ascertain whether these changes signalled radical or merely superficial progress for women. As with previous evaluations, you should be aware that further emancipation could only be secured if there was a reform in underlying attitudes towards women's role in society. You should therefore establish the extent to which both women and men supported the developments that arose during the war. Return to the topics suggested above and note down what evidence you can find of a breakdown in traditional views as well as the evidence which favours continuity in opinions. Refer to the differing views of historians and see if you can develop your own conclusions. As a final test of your understanding of the chapter, see if you can in note form answer the questions raised in each of the key issues.

Source-based questions on Chapter 5

1. Attitudes towards Women
Read the extract by Edith Summerskill on page 89, the extract entitled 'Woman's Place' on pages 89–90, and look at the recruitment poster on page 90.

a) What does Summerskill mean by 'preconceived ideas' (line 4)? (*3 marks*)
b) Why did the author of 'Woman's Place' attack 'upper-class feminists' (line 1)? (*3 marks*)
c) With reference to the recruitment poster and using your own knowledge, how important was propaganda in influencing attitudes towards women during the war? (*6 marks*)
d) How useful are these sources in explaining attitudes towards women in the Second World War? (*8 marks*)

Hints and advice: Both Questions 1a) and b) test comprehension of sources, but this is very dependent on the extent to which you have understood key arguments in the chapter. Re-read relevant sections, if necessary. Question 1c) asks you to think not only about the poster but the context in which it was produced. For example, why did propaganda have to be used in relation to women during the war? Finally, for Question 1d) you will need to evaluate both the individual source for utility as well as looking at the broader picture of whether they help to explain attitudes towards women.

6 Post-war Britain, 1945–68: a New Era?

POINTS TO CONSIDER

During this period of post-war recovery a number of conflicting and often confusing influences helped to shape the direction of women's lives in Britain. As you read this chapter, try to understand the implications for women of the resurgence of a more conservative feminism as well as the effects of the more liberalising attitudes of the 'swinging sixties'. In particular, you should identify the different criteria defining women's lives after 1945 and, with this knowledge, try to appreciate why feminism was poised to embrace the idea of the women's liberation movement after 1968.

KEY DATES

1945	**8 May**	Armistice with Germany.
		Control of Employment Act.
1946		Royal Commission on Equal Pay.
		National Insurance Act and National Health Service Act passed.
		Death of Eleanor Rathbone.
1947		Death of Ellen Wilkinson.
1956		Morton Commission on Divorce.
1957		National Council for the Abolition of Nuclear Weapons founded.
1958	**Jan**	Campaign for Nuclear Disarmament launched.
		Lambeth Conference of the Church of England.
		Life Peerages Act passed.
1963		Peeresses admitted to House of Lords in their own right.
1967		Abortion Act.
1968		50th Anniversary of Women's Suffrage.
		Women sewing machinists on strike at Ford Dagenham plant.

1 Introduction

> **KEY ISSUE** What were the key factors shaping the lives of women in Britain after 1945?

In 1945, women discovered that the potential progress which they had experienced during the war was now curtailed by a male-directed agenda. This manifested itself in several ways. Although women had participated on a large scale in the workforce, they still lacked real economic power. Thus the underlying tendency to discriminate against women in jobs was sustained after 1945 on the grounds that men were intended to be the primary providers for the family.

Yet women were soon the recipients of conflicting messages. Unlike 1918 when unemployment became a serious problem, in 1945 the government was soon faced with manpower shortages due to demands on industry. Women were its one remaining source of untapped labour. Hence women were encouraged to return to work, albeit on a part-time rather than a full-time basis. But the traditional view of family life based on a culture of domesticity still prevailed and had a major impact on the way women's roles in post-war society would develop. With the implementation of the Beveridge Report and the introduction of the National Health Service, the government made an explicit statement regarding its future plans for women. Such plans were also reflected in education policies which endorsed a strong focus on domestic science within the curriculum for girls. The consequence of these policies meant that women increasingly assumed a dual role – wage earner and home maker.

Within politics, women continued to be poorly represented due to on-going prejudice especially at constituency level towards women MPs. However, in the 1960s women made more of an impact within the Commons partly as a result of several key promotions made by prime minister, Harold Wilson. It was in that decade too that women started to reverse some of the stereotyped images of themselves. Encouraged by some forthright feminist analysis of the status of women within society, plus a series of acts of parliament protecting their rights, women were finally questioning current definitions of femininity. Whereas an image of passivity and dependency, an image largely manipulated by men's own ideal of women, had dominated since 1945, by the late 1960s women were gaining greater self-confidence, a change which was due in part to greater affluence plus the wider availability of birth control.

2 Changing Work Patterns

KEY ISSUE How did the pattern of work for women change after 1945?

a) Women's Status within the Workforce

Before the conclusion of the war, many women were already experiencing the likely developments in peacetime employment patterns. From 1943 onwards, the numbers employed in the munitions factories were reduced, thus setting a trend which continued after 1945. Despite their valuable contributions to the war effort, women discovered that trade union leaders barely resisted dismissal of female employees. Their loyalties rested with the returning male servicemen. In similar circumstances to 1918 (see page 55), under the Control of Employment Act of 1945 demobilised women seeking work at the

Labour Exchanges were given less priority than men. Indeed, as the army was demobilised, traditional attitudes towards women resurfaced. Married women especially were told explicitly that they had no right to deprive a man of a job when he had a family to support. Overall, the number of women employed decreased by 1,750,000 between 1943 and 1947. Whereas in 1943 51 per cent of all adult women worked, this figure had been reduced to 40 per cent by 1947.[1]

Although it suited government, employers, trade unionists and male employees to channel women back into the home, this ideology soon proved ineffective. Whilst most women agreed that they should stay at home with young children, declining numbers were prepared to tolerate the boredom of being at home all day. Then, by 1947 continuing labour shortages forced the Ministry of Labour to launch an appeal to encourage women to work in industry if they could. Employers reluctantly signed on married women, viewing this as a necessary expedient to overcome a short-term problem. Married women were always the first group to suffer dismissal. Nevertheless their role as an essential component within the nation's workforce was re-established. The shift in employment patterns which had accelerated during the war was not reversed. Between 1947 and 1957 there was an increase amongst married women working from 18 per cent to around 30 per cent.

What types of work did women do? In her survey of married women workers published in 1965[2] (see below), Viola Klein concluded that factory workers were the largest occupational group amongst married women.

Types of Work	Married Women Working			Single Women
	Full-time	Part-time	Total	Total
Domestic workers, cleaners, canteen/school meal helpers	15	45	31	10
Factory workers	22	10	16	14
Shop assistants	15	12	13	15
Clerical, office workers	10	15	13	19
Business: supervisory grades (shop managers etc.)	14	3	8	7
Teachers, librarians, professional workers	7	5	6	10
Personal services (e.g. receptionists hairdressers, dressmakers etc.)	6	4	5	7
Secretaries, typists etc.	8	1	4	14
Other types of work	2	4	3	2
Not stated	1	1	1	2

Working Women by Type of Occupation (percentages)

A considerable number of those jobs were in the newer industries such as food processing, synthetic fibres, and light electrical goods. Amongst part-time workers, domestic work was the highest source of employment. Klein's survey provided firm evidence that the overwhelming trend after 1945 was for women to be concentrated in unskilled or semi-skilled jobs. Regardless of whether women worked part-time or not, 60 per cent of all working women did unskilled work.[3] Further illustration of the nature of women's work emerged in a survey conducted by the Six Point Group published in 1968 which showed that some 75 per cent of all women employed were occupied in jobs which took less than six months to master.[4]

Within the higher ranks of industry as well as professional levels there was a scarcity of women. Ministry of Labour figures from 1964 revealed that women made up only five per cent of managers in science and technology, nine per cent of dentists, less than five per cent of those in the legal profession, eight per cent of top grade civil servants although 25 per cent were medical practitioners.[5] The only professions to be dominated by women were teaching where labour shortages had prompted calls for women to resume their careers (58.8 per cent were women) and nursing (90.2 per cent).

Alongside gender segregation in work, women also had to accept lower wages than men. Campaigns for equal pay had only limited success, since the 1945–51 Labour government viewed increases in women's pay as inflationary at a time of post-war economic austerity. In 1946 a Royal Commission on Equal Pay had reported, but it only recommended equal pay for the lower grades in the Civil Service, teaching and local government. The London County Council finally conceded equal pay for teachers, nurses and clerical workers in 1952, to be followed by implementation nationwide between 1954 and 1962. These were significant achievements but in most other occupations lower pay structures applied to women. In 1966 the average weekly pay for women was just 49 per cent of a man's wage. As long as women's primary role was deemed to be that of wife and mother, rather than pursuing a career, women's status within the workplace would continue to be marginalised.

b) Causes of Women's Employment Patterns

How can the obvious failings of women to redress long-term patterns of employment be explained? One insight can be gained from women's own attitudes towards work. Most women still envisaged their vocation as being that of wife and mother. Training for a career was largely superfluous because work was merely a transitory stage in their life before settling down to bring up a family. Low educational expectations of girls also aggravated their lack of long-term career ambitions. As Elizabeth Roberts noted:

1   Many of the features of young women's work can be illustrated by the
     assumptions they made about their lives. Girls' ambitions did not centre
     on work, but on marriage and children. Work may have been enjoyable,
     but it was not seen as a lifetime commitment. Fifteen-year-old girls
5   envisaged a job with or without training, then marriage with a continu-
     ation of paid work until the birth of the first child. The great majority
     could see no further than that. Young men had different expectations:
     they left school assuming they would work until they were sixty-five
     years old.[6]

External factors also influenced this culture of domesticity. Women
were often prevented from pursuing a wide range of occupations by
employers many of whom believed that women were best suited to
'feminine' types of work such as teaching and nursing or jobs involving manual dexterity. It was not surprising that so many well-educated, intelligent women progressed no further than the post of
secretary, despite having the potential to be an effective executive.
Furthermore, women were caught in a vicious circle whereby they
were urged to help tackle the labour shortages, but then attacked for
what was deemed an increase in juvenile delinquency amongst children whose mothers worked (see page 109). Thus, as Alva Myrdal and
Viola Klein noted in 1956, the dilemmas for women would continue:

> until society has so adjusted itself, mentally and materially, to the new
> conditions that it will be possible for women satisfactorily to combine
> the pursuit of a chosen career with marriage and family life.[7]

Until that happened, women would be torn between the emotional
pull of motherhood and the more practical considerations of work.
    Nevertheless, as more married women returned to work, three
chronological phases in a woman's life were now apparent: i) longer
years in education followed by gainful employment, ii) marriage and
iii) post-motherhood. It was this last phase which attracted the attention of contemporary observers. Given that women spent fewer years
on child-rearing (see below), how should women now occupy their
time, especially as they faced approximately 20 further years before
retirement?

c) Why Did Women Return to Work?

The motives for seeking work were varied, although two key factors
seemed to dominate. In the immediate aftermath of the war housewives had felt oppressed by the continuing economic austerity policies of the government. Rationing had persisted as part of a stringent
programme of national economies. But once this ended, a boom in
consumer goods took off, tempting the housewife with the latest time-
saving household gadgets which would, in theory, make housework
less onerous. There was also a realisation that increased income

created opportunities for a decent holiday, better education for the children or to purchase a car. A higher standard of living, therefore, became a compelling motive for working. The second incentive was to escape from the loneliness of the home environment. Professional women returning to the Civil Service regarded work as a means of gaining a higher standard of living and companionship. Klein's survey also confirmed that women wanted to escape from household drudgery and enhance their lifestyles.

1 I get fed up and morbid spending nearly all day alone; I feel it would keep me younger having a job (age 48, one child).
   It would just give me an extra interest in life. As one gets older, life seems to get emptier (age 59).
5 Oh, it would be smashing to get a break. To get away from this lot for an hour or two – it would be like heaven! (age 32, 9 children).
   For the extras, clothes mostly and get taken out of myself (30, 2 children).[8]

Several conclusions can be drawn from the various studies conducted on the nature of women's work during the period from 1945 to 1968. The most encouraging trend was that more women sought and accepted the value of working outside the home. To a certain degree, this symbolised greater economic emancipation. Inevitably, in conjunction with this development, women exhibited greater self-confidence. Less encouraging was the fact that women's work was invariably determined by gender. Women were channelled into low-skilled, part-time jobs because of on-going discrimination and the practical problems of combining work and home. They still lacked the economic clout with which to counteract prevailing attitudes towards women's place in the workforce.

3 The Welfare State

> **KEY ISSUE** How did the introduction of the welfare state change the lives of women?

Following the disruptions of the war, the government was anxious to create an appropriate climate in which the stability of the family could be restored. The introduction of the 1946 National Insurance Act and the National Health Service Act, which came into force in 1948, represented a significant advance in terms of promoting basic health care and welfare provisions for women and children. But the continued dependency of women upon their husbands was enshrined within the terms of the acts. Despite twenty years of equal suffrage, women were still denied equality within the family.

In many respects the new welfare state discriminated against women. Married women were categorised as dependants of their husbands.

Non-working housewives were unable to claim independently because they were covered by their husband's insurance. Those who did work were not compelled to contribute to the national insurance scheme because they were deemed part of a 'husband and wife' team. If a woman opted to contribute, she received 25 per cent less in sickness and unemployment benefits than her husband. Single women were permitted to make contributions but their benefits were at a lower rate mainly because the government chose not to recognise that such women might have to support dependants. The main direction of the system was to encourage women to sustain their domestic responsibilities rather than seek full-time work.

However, for women with families the new welfare state did bring several advantages. Family allowances were introduced in August 1946, a satisfactory but long overdue conclusion to Eleanor Rathbone's persistent campaigning. Following protests by women MPs, five shillings (25p) a week was paid directly to the mother rather than the father for the second and every subsequent child, although this was a lower rate than originally hoped. Further assistance was granted to pregnant women, who got 13 weeks' maternity benefit; this enabled a mother to give up work both before and after the birth of her child. Widows' pensions were also improved.

The introduction of the National Health Service (NHS) was designed to tackle the poor state of health suffered by all those who could not afford medical insurance. Under the pre-war system, thousands of women had endured repeated ill health, especially in relation to pregnancy and post-natal complications. For the first time, the idea of free universal health care, a fundamental principle of the welfare state, was incorporated within government legislation. The combination of free hospital treatment and health care from general practitioners and dentists represented a major development in addressing the nation's health problems. For women, the long-term impact of these reforms was significant, with notable improvements occurring in neo-infant and maternal mortality rates. Whereas previously women often sought free medical advice from family or friends, now they were far more inclined to gain professional medical opinion.

One aspect of Beveridge's plans, however, was not successfully enacted. A key objective of the Welfare State had been to enhance the attractions of family life. Beveridge realised that most middle-class families were now deprived of their domestic infrastructure – nanny, cook and housemaid; so in order to alleviate the burden on the housewife, he had outlined plans for community laundry facilities and other domestic chores. He did not want the tired housewife to become a slave within her home. But fears that these measures were too socialist, plus the need for government economies, forced the abandonment of such plans.

During the period of post-war austerity, the introduction of the Welfare State signified a concern to provide a safety net against the worst forms of poverty. It also symbolised the new Britain which the Labour government sought to create. Opponents, however, criticised the increased levels of state intervention. When the Conservatives replaced Labour in 1951 wages were beginning to rise. As a result, the Conservatives invested less in the Welfare State. For women, this meant that their status within the new welfare system would continue to be subsidiary to that of men.

4 Education Policies

KEY ISSUES What were the key influences affecting educational policies for girls after 1945? To what extent did educational opportunities expand for girls during this period?

a) Post-war Educational Ideas

In 1945, the resumption of peace provided the new Labour government with an opportunity to formulate policies which would shape the future of Britain. In that respect, education would be a key factor in determining women's function within modern society.

Early indication of current thinking was revealed in 1948, when John Newsom published an important investigation into the nature of girls' education. *The Education of Girls* encapsulated much of contemporary thought by asserting that girls had separate functions to boys in life and had to be prepared accordingly. His ideas provided the necessary endorsement for government policies on women, namely that a woman's main occupation was marriage rather than a long-term career.

> ... for the vast majority of women, the business of homemaking and the early nurture of children is a dominant theme in their lives, while for men the equivalent dominant is to earn enough to support their wives and families.[9]

Newsom upheld employers' beliefs that it was unnecessary to train girls for highly skilled or responsible jobs. So much of industrial work required semi-skilled operatives who could tolerate repetitive work. Women, he claimed, were both content to do this work and accept the accompanying wages. The danger of better education would be to make them less acquiescent. Newsom attacked the current curriculum because it had been determined by the needs of a minority, essentially those attending grammar schools, and had failed to accommodate the fact that a majority of girls 'will become the makers of homes'. He continued,

> With notable exceptions, it is true to say that the education of girls has been modelled on that of their brothers without any reference to their different function in society. This is a modern perversion and its

corrupting influence dates from the end of the last century, when the
5 pioneers of a higher education for women finally secured 'equal
opportunities' for girls. Until their triumph the education of girls had
been to a considerable extent related to their needs and the needs of
society. Unfortunately, the reformers were impelled to condemn
everything that had been done before them, in order to emphasize the
10 virtues of their particular cause. It became orthodox to denigrate the
domestic virtues and the very word 'mid-Victorian', when applied to
women, has become a form of abuse.[10]

Newsom's report appeared four years after the 1944 Education Act
(see page 107) which had introduced free, secondary education,
including grammar schools, to all children up to 15 years. Newsom
feared that firstly, there might be attempts to implement a grammar
school style education at all levels and secondly, that this would
undermine previous education policies which had encouraged, for
girls of average ability, a fairly restricted curriculum. He favoured
limited vocational training which would include a knowledge of nutrition, housekeeping, simple account keeping, competence in needlework and dressmaking as well as an awareness of the importance of
sanitation. His advocacy of a prescribed vocational training had a definite impact on educational expectations for girls.

Two reports published in 1959 indicated little progress in terms of
educational thinking over the previous decade. The Central Advisory
Council for Education (England) issued a report which noted that,
'Though the general objectives of secondary education remain
unchanged, [a girl's] direct interest in dress, personal appearance and
in problems of human relations should be given a central place in her
education'.[11] Another evaluation, the Crowther Report, had focused
on the education of girls aged 15-18. Whilst it accepted the need for
intellectual girls to go to university, ambitions for less able girls
remained modest. For them, clerical work or shopkeeping seemed
more appropriate. Such expectations were on a par with those con-
templated for working-class boys or newly-arrived black immigrants.

Only in the 1960s did the education debate begin to offer a more
critical examination of girls' education. This took place within the
context of changing expectations for girls especially amongst many
parents, helped by improvements in family incomes, the accumulative
effect of universal free secondary education since 1944, and the post-
war expansion in university education. As the economy improved,
there was less pressure to leave school and get a job. Greater value was
therefore placed on education.

A Working Party set up by the National Council of Social Service in
1962 undertook a very thorough investigation of girls' education. It
highlighted the dissatisfaction of professional women who, after several years of academic study and professional training, were often
forced to relinquish their careers because of the strains of dual

responsibilities. But its recommendations placed a more positive emphasis on the importance of women reaching their full potential. There was a clear recognition that girls should be encouraged to pursue more ambitious educational objectives. In its recommendations the report stated:

1   We urge Her Majesty's Government:
    (a) the education of girls should at all levels give the same opportunities of intellectual advancement as are available to boys;
    (b) every effort should be made to improve the facilities for teaching
5   mathematics and science in girls' schools ...
    (f) schools should give even more attention to advising girls about suitable careers and opportunities for employment, reminding them that, although they may marry young, they will probably want to return to some form of work later in life and should prepare themselves accordingly.[12]

It was the most forward-looking educational document to emerge from the post-war era and certainly helped to promote the development of a more equitable system of education for girls.

b) Post-War Education for Girls

The 1944 Education Act represented a major step forward in the provision of education in Britain. Prior to 1944, 30 per cent of both boys and girls were still attending the overcrowded elementary schools (see page 00) rather than acquiring official secondary education. The 1944 Act, however, stipulated that local education authorities were obliged to provide secondary education for all children aged 11–15. There was also the stated intention to raise the school leaving age to 16, although this was not implemented until the academic year 1970–71.

In many respects the curriculum for girls reflected contemporary policies in that an explicit emphasis on liberal arts and domestic science prevailed. Despite concerns by the 1960s to rectify this imbalance, the cyclical effect of educational thought, low educational expectations, limited career opportunities and a shortage of women teachers in mathematics, physics and chemistry meant that marked differences in subjects taken by girls and boys were sustained. In choosing predominantly arts subjects and modern languages, girls could not help but be influenced by the assumptions that they had different interests from boys. Arguments that girls found algebra and geometry more difficult seemed to be reflected in the fact that in 1959 twice as many boys as girls took mathematics 'O' Level. Even smaller proportions of girls took physics and chemistry, whereas more sat exams in religious education, history and geography.

The post-war educational system promoted a practical curriculum for girls in line with current disquiet about the inappropriate effects of an academic schooling. Secondary modern schools, attended by

70–75 per cent of the school population, concentrated on a vocational educational programme which prepared girls for their dual role in life. Proficiency in the art of homemaking was encouraged, with domestic science fully integrated in the curriculum rather than girls being sent, as had happened pre-war, to separate training centres. Typing was also popular, given that clerical work was one of the most likely sources of employment for girls leaving school with just 'O' Level passes.

The problem with emphasising a two-tier system of education was that the disparities between education for the able and less able and between girls and boys became even more glaring. As general expectations of educational provision rose, so concerns were heightened that girls were lacking the same opportunities as boys. The inadequate supply of female teachers in mathematics and science could only be addressed, for example, if more girls took those subjects at 'A' Level, and studied them at university (fewer than one fifth studied those subjects in 1961). The expansion of universities in the 1960s did facilitate admissions of women to higher education, but women still tended to select arts subjects for their degrees. For girls' education to experience any significant change, a number of conditions would need to be met, not least a practical solution to the gender defined education of girls, and a widening of employment opportunities which would encourage girls to extend their choice of careers.

5 Women and the Family

> **KEY ISSUES** To what extent did perceptions of women's role within the family change? Did post-war developments enhance or deter the social emancipation of women?

As the sections on employment, the Welfare State and education have suggested, the prevailing ideology of the 40s and 50s was one which encouraged a life of domesticity for women. By the 60s, however, many women had begun to question that rather prescribed image. Women's status within the family was affected by many key developments which, in conjunction with more liberalised attitudes, helped to break down some of women's more traditional experiences.

a) Children

In the first half of the century children had, for many women, been regarded primarily as an economic responsibility – food, clothing, housing had to be provided, but as soon as they could become independent, offspring were dispatched to earn a living. However, within the post-war climate of promoting motherhood, the notion that childcare was merely a functional task within marriage began to change.

The whole psychology of child development was transformed by a range of literature which highlighted a more child-centred approach to children's upbringing. Relieved of some of the physical burdens of housework, women were urged to allocate more time to focusing on the key developmental stages of childhood. The importance of 'mother love' and the detrimental effects of maternal deprivation were explored in John Bowlby's book *Child Care and the Growth of Love* (1953). Bowlby presented a powerful argument asserting that long-term damage would result if a mother abrogated her maternal duties during the first three years of a child's life. Given that few women could rely on a nanny for help, the mother bore sole responsibility for her child and, exhorted by magazines to be the perfect parent, could not be seen to be neglecting its health and happiness.

Furthermore anxious mothers, uncertain how to cope on their own with minor illnesses, eating problems or tantrums, could resort to the growing number of child-care manuals which purported to provide authoritative advice, such as Dr. Benjamin Spock's *Common Sense Book of Baby and Child Care* (1946). These books, in conjunction with the increased level of state intervention in children's physical development, such as regular checks at a child health clinic, all contributed to the new trends in child care. What the manuals failed to address, however, was the growing sense of isolation and frustration that some women felt as a result of being confined to the home.

Although more women were undertaking work, especially as their children got older, it was still difficult to combine the dual role of home and work. Lack of nurseries or cover arrangements for school holidays forced women to work part-time. Moreover, employers were not ready to adjust work schedules to accommodate family needs. The fact that women did work, however, also provoked heated debate about the link between increased child delinquency and maternal employment. Allegations that there was a direct causal effect provided further stimulus to the belief that women should stay at home. Although a report by Terence Moore, *Working Mothers and their Children* (1963), refuted any correlation between these two factors, many women felt guilty if they sought work.

It was in the 60s, though, that some women began to criticise what had become a glamorised image of motherhood. Writers such as Penelope Mortimer and Margaret Drabble both wrote newspaper articles in which they deplored the gloss placed on child rearing when in reality women endured much hardship and social isolation. As the feminist movement moved into a new era of liberalised attitudes and behaviour (see Section 6b), so it became more acceptable to question the belief that women could only be fulfilled through motherhood.

b) Marriage, Divorce, Birth Control and Abortion

After 1945, marriage continued to be regarded as a woman's main vocation in life. In 1931, 41.3 per cent of all women were married, as opposed to being single, widowed or divorced, whereas by 1951 this had risen to 48.7 per cent. Marriage was sought, as had been the case before the war, more for reasons of personal happiness than purely economic considerations. But happiness was defined by a very stereotyped view of the woman's role. Magazines such as *Woman* combined practical advice on cooking healthy meals with tips on how to make oneself attractive to one's husband. The introduction of convenience foods such as canned vegetables helped to transform diets but also relieved the housewife of some of the tedium of cooking, as the advertisement for Batchelors foods reveals (see the page opposite).

As suggested above, many women experienced increasing social isolation. Close-knit communities, which had so often been a life-support for wives, providing social contact and neighbourly advice, were broken up by post-war housing developments. This, plus the introduction of television, meant that families became more insular. Although more men shared domestic tasks at home they, unlike their wives, could escape from home life by going to the pub or working men's club. Such options were not available to women.

The public image of marriage was one which often glamorised married life. In such a climate it could be difficult to admit to sexual problems within a marriage. During the 40s and 50s women were expected to tolerate marital difficulties even if they amounted to infidelity. Nevertheless, the government was increasingly concerned that women were more inclined to seek divorce as a solution to their problems. Consternation about changing attitudes was reflected in the Morton Commission on Divorce (1956) which attacked the way husbands and wives were 'lacking in a sense of duty and responsibilities to each other and to their children'.[13]

Eventually the 1969 Divorce Act was passed, its main merit being to simplify divorce proceedings by establishing the principle of 'no fault' divorce whereas previously one partner had to prove grounds for divorce. This, together with a more positive approach by courts to the economic welfare of women and children, encouraged an escalation in the termination of difficult marriages.

Year	Divorce rate per 1000
1951	2.6
1961	2.1
1971	6.0

Another important development for women was the recognition by the Lambeth Conference of the Church of England in 1958 that family planning should be an integral part of a Christian couple's married life. This was acceptance that sexual pleasure within a marriage was as legitimate as procreation and that a couple should be

"So this is Love!" Of course, George loves me. But sometimes it's very hard to believe. For instance, when he 'phones from the office that he's bringing business friends home to dinner. What do I do? I rely on Batchelors canned foods to make the meal a real success and big enough for all . . .

able to choose when to start a family. Then in 1961 contraception was transformed by the introduction of the Pill, although its availability was somewhat limited until it became free on the NHS in 1969. The simplicity of taking the Pill compared with using a condom or the cap meant that women could now separate sexual pleasure from reproduction. This had enormous implications for women's perceptions of themselves in that they could envisage greater sexual equality both within and outside marriage. In 1938, the Family Planning Association had operated 61 clinics, by 1948 it had 65, but this had increased to 400 by 1963. As the more permissive society of the sixties emerged, critics attacked the Pill for causing an increase in pre-marital sex. For women, however, it widened their choice in how to conduct their lives.

One final indicator as to the extent to which women had become more emancipated emerged when, amidst much controversy, the Abortion Act was passed in October 1967. Fierce debate had surrounded the passage of this bill with advocates arguing for the 'choice of motherhood' and 'equality of women' whilst opponents, in particular Catholics, asserted that all life was sacred. The Act permitted abortion up to 28 weeks if pregnancy posed a physical or mental health risk to the mother or a risk to the welfare of other children or if there was a serious danger that the child might be born seriously handicapped. One of the interesting motives behind the supporters of the bill had been a heightened social concern, namely society's inadequate care of unwanted, handicapped children. Although the terms under which an abortion might be permitted seemed quite restricted, the Act was a milestone in facilitating women's management of their personal lives.

6 Developments in Feminism

> **KEY ISSUE** How did the image of women change after the war?

In the Second World War, women had gained some semblance of equality in that they were involved in the affairs of the nation, they worked and they managed their families. But after 1945, such potential gains were undermined by the resurgence of traditional attitudes towards women. As discussed above, women were targeted from all angles to resume their roles as housewives. How, then, did the image of women develop thereafter?

a) The 1940s and 1950s

In 1947, Christian Dior launched his famous 'New Look' design. Rebelling against dreary utility wartime clothes, Dior opened the cage door of fashion and captured women's imaginations. But his dress designs of tiny waists, padded bosoms and hips, and large full skirts created an image of woman as being elegant and totally 'feminine'. It accorded well with much of the thinking which underlay public policies towards women. A life at home might indeed feel glamorous if one could dress the part as well.

> The stars of Hollywood also contributed to the evolving images of women. On the one hand there was the cool, poised figure of Grace Kelly; on the other the sexy, kittenish Marilyn Monroe, blonde but vulnerable. Monroe herself admitted, 'I think it's terribly important to feel feminine, to act feminine ... Men *need* women to be feminine'.[14]

With such strong prevailing public portrayals of femininity, it was little wonder that those within the women's movement struggled to make any significant advances after 1945. Indeed experienced feminists were now disappointed by women's failure to challenge traditional divisions of labour between the sexes. Instead, post-war feminists focused their campaigns on improving social conditions and on ame-liorating the more arduous features of family life. They even endorsed women's supposed special qualities, homemaking and mothering. Hence it was a matter of assisting women to accommodate the dilemmas of children and work, rather than tackling the causes of economic and social injustices. Women could be equal but different to men. Continued dependency on men was not challenged. The aims of feminism during the 1940s and 1950s, therefore, were nar-rower, tempered by women's perceptions of themselves as well as embedded attitudes within society.

The limited goals of various women's organisations exemplified the nature of the women's movement. The British Housewives League campaigned against Labour's food rationing policy after 1945 but it was not driven by feminist aims. Numerous women's groups affiliated to the National Council of Women; two of its conferences, one on single women in 1955 and another on working mothers in 1958, illustrate the kind of issues that predominated. The SPG and the WFL (see pages 46 and 36) remained the most radical of all the organisations but they were still campaigning for an agenda set in the 1920s: equal pay, an end to discrimination in work practices. There was little attempt to develop any new approaches to the issues con-cerning women. They were further handicapped by the fact that they were unable to recruit new young members. One organisation, how-ever, which did capture the imagination of many women was the National Council for the Abolition of Nuclear Weapons, founded in 1957 and which was the precursor to the Campaign for Nuclear Disarmament (CND). This signified a new social movement involving housewives and mothers, many of whom had had little previous com-mitment to any one cause. Together they shared a concern about the implications of nuclear weapons for their families. Although more radical individuals were also members, the early inclusion of ordinary women marked a new stage in women's association with the peace movement, culminating in the emergence of the Greenham Common protests in the 1980s.

b) The 1960s

The 1960s marked a transitional period for feminism during which passive images of femininity gave way to a more relaxed, morally unconstrained impression of feminism. Several developments pro-vided the momentum for change.

First, there was the combined impact of new exciting styles in music and fashion. Young people were caught up by the swinging music of the 60s – rhythm, blues, the Beatles, Gerry and the Pacemakers – which seemed to evoke a sense of rebellion and non-conformity. In fashion, the tall, thin, waif like figure of the model Twiggy with her short cropped hair represented a complete antithe-

Twiggy

sis to the glamorous, romantic but sexy image of Marilyn Monroe who had typified 1950s femininity. Mary Quant geometric hair styles, mini skirts, white lipstick and black eyeliner were all symptomatic of a desire to break with convention.

Convention was challenged in other respects. The decade commenced with the famous trial in 1961 of D.H. Lawrence's *Lady Chatterley's Lover* in which the publishers Penguin were charged under the Obscene Publications Act of 1959. The significance of Penguin's victory in the courts went beyond the rights of a publisher to print an explicit novel. Now there was public rather than discreet recognition that sexual pleasure need not occur merely within the confines of marriage. Further scandal emerged in 1963 when the Minister for Defence, John Profumo, was caught in a relationship with a prostitute, Christine Keeler.

1   Suddenly people could talk abut sex because it was in the news, – Christine Keeler, Lady Chatterley case, – ordinary, respectable, married women could sit round dinner tables and talk about it. It wasn't the Big Secret. But it was the Pill, I think, that made it possible for things to
5   change, for women to find out about themselves.[15]

The reform of women's self image gained further impetus from feminist writings. Betty Friedan's *The Feminine Mystique* (1963) shattered the vision of domestic contentment which women were purported to enjoy. Friedan gave voice to the thousands of women who had been too afraid to admit that they were unfulfilled by family routines. Instead, she advocated that every woman had a right to a separate identity.

> Even a very young woman today must think of herself as a human being first, not as a mother with time on her hands, and make a life plan in terms of her own abilities, a commitment of her own to society, with which her commitments as wife and mother can be integrated.[16]

On a similar theme, Hannah Gavron's *The Captive Wife* (1966) claimed that women were imprisoned by home life and lack of an occupation. She rejected the contention made by Bowlby in the 1950s that working mothers damaged their children.

Finally, Juliet Mitchell's article 'Women: the Longest Revolution' (1966) was one of several catalysts that helped to precipitate the Women's Liberation Movement in 1970. In her article, she attacked the 'monolithic characteristic of marriage', arguing that women's role within the family had to be freed from the oppression of unwanted reproduction. Capturing the more permissive atmosphere of the late 60s, Mitchell contended that there should be a diversification of relationships away from the stereotype relationship of married man and woman. Women's emancipation rested not only on breaking away from marital conventions but also in seeking equal work and equal education.

Radicalism therefore was manifested in several ways. CND provided a continued focus for women as did the emerging student political protests of the late 60s. But two events in 1968 served as a sharp reminder that women still faced many obstacles. The first was the fact that 1968 was the 50th anniversary of women's suffrage. Half a century of political rights had still not gained women equality. The second was the strike by women sewing machinists at Ford's Dagenham factory for equal pay (see page 124). This strike conveyed a new sense of militancy which was infectious. As the Women's Liberation Movement took hold in America, women in Britain began to question whether they had really been liberated by the permissiveness of the 60s. There was a growing sense that if women wanted to change their lives, they would have to act alone.

7 Politics

> **KEY ISSUE** How far could women be satisfied with their progress in politics after 50 years of political rights?

During the war, women's political profile had been raised because they had acted as a cohesive group within Parliament, forcing the government to give serious consideration to women's issues. But how far were women MPs able to sustain that momentum after the war?

a) The Road to Parliament

Many of the problems which had thwarted women's political progress prior to 1939 still applied in the postwar period, the net impact of which could be seen in the number of women elected to the House of Commons: 24 MPs in 1945, and in 1968 only 27 MPs. Numbers obviously fluctuated in the interim, but for so little overall progress to have been made was a sad reflection of the status of women in politics, 50 years after first gaining the vote. Why did women find it so difficult to break down gender barriers?

The selection process within the constituencies proved the first hurdle. Women still encountered considerable prejudice from those on the selection panel, including members of their own sex. Within the Labour Party women had to compete against union-sponsored candidates who held the advantage of guaranteed funds and a network of support. Conservatives often preferred a married man because they would automatically gain his wife's help with constituency work. A married woman was less likely to possess a free, supportive husband. Huge scepticism also greeted the married woman with children as few selectors believed that she could devote enough time to a political career. If the family home was located far from the constituency, then a woman faced further problems in convincing selectors that she could be sufficiently mobile to manage constituency affairs. As a result, women were less likely to be selected to fight a winnable seat. In 1964, for example, 70 per cent of all women candidates were contesting seats where they faced overturning an opposition majority of over 5,000 votes. Victory would necessitate a large swing in votes. In order to get selected, a woman had to have outstanding qualities, including high motivation and determination. Prejudice, however, was less apparent amongst voters who, once presented with a female candidate, did not express widespread opposition to the concept of a woman MP.

Life at Westminster and the atmosphere within the Commons continued to deter women from politics. In 1968, the salary was £3,250 per annum from which board and lodgings near Westminster had to be funded. The long hours of parliamentary sittings remained unaltered, so it was hard to sustain normal family life. Although most women MPs were married or widowed, few possessed children of school age or younger when elected. One exception was Margaret Thatcher who, aged 32 and as a mother of five-year-old twins, was elected in 1959.

Women also discovered that men dominated the political machinery at Westminster. Male MPs could network through the male-dominated trade unions, whereas women were largely excluded. Within the Labour Party, women had their own section, the National Labour Women's Advisory Committee which held its own annual conference, plus they had five seats on the National Executive Committee. However, Labour women were critical of a system which gave them a separate platform, the implication being that they were not deemed competent to speak on the same platform and about the same issues as men. But in one respect women did hold an advantage over men. A higher percentage of women elected gained ministerial office, which suggests that governments appreciated that the inclusion of women would improve their image.

b) Women's Success Inside Parliament

After 1945, the women who had dominated pre-war politics and who had fought so determinedly for women's issues were gradually supplanted by a fresh intake of women whose goals and ideals were shaped by different perspectives. One notable absentee in 1945 was Lady Astor who retired from politics because, as she admitted, her husband did not wish her to fight another election. Amongst the new influx of MPs were Alice Bacon, Margaret Herbison and Barbara Castle (who was only 34 years old). What distinguished these and subsequent women was the fact that they were less inclined to regard their role as one of primarily defending women's issues within the Commons. They wished to be recognised for their political skills rather than their sex.

Nevertheless, political leaders still ascribed women MPs with expertise in women's issues and appointed them accordingly. In Attlee's government of 1945 Ellen Wilkinson became Minister of Education with a seat in the Cabinet, Dr. Edith Summerskill was Parliamentary Secretary to the Minister of Food and Jennie Adamson was Parliamentary Secretary to the Minister of Pensions. Together with other experienced women politicians, they adhered to the traditional approach of defending special interests. Edith Summerskill successfully secured the Milk (Special Designation) Bill in 1949 which made it compulsory to pasteurise milk or test it for tuberculosis. Other subjects which attracted the attention of women MPs were post-war housing, the National Health Service and the care and adoption of children.

In subsequent Labour and Conservative governments, women continued to have some impact. Irene Ward returned to Parliament in 1950 whereupon she resumed her campaign to secure equal pay. It was due to her persistent questioning in the Commons that R.A. Butler, the Conservative Chancellor of the Exchequer, promised to fulfil an election pledge to introduce equal pay for the Civil Service and local government in 1954. Although women were still appointed to departments which were supposedly close to women's issues – Florence Horsbrugh as Minister of Education under Churchill in

1951 and Pat Hornsby-Smith as Parliamentary Secretary at the Ministry of Health under Anthony Eden and then at the Home Office under Harold Macmillan – increasingly women established a reputation for speaking authoritatively on other issues. Barbara Castle in particular made notable attacks on the Conservative government's handling of the Mau Mau tribal unrest in Kenya in 1959.

The major breakthrough for women occurred under Harold Wilson's leadership in 1964 when seven out of 18 women were given posts in his government. Barbara Castle first became Minister of Overseas Development and then, more radically, the Minister for Transport in January 1966. Alice Bacon was Minister of State at the Home Office and Margaret Herbison Minister of Pensions and National Insurance. Margaret Thatcher, meanwhile, was the opposition spokesperson for the Treasury and economic affairs. The other key development for women occurred in the Upper House whose anachronistic, exclusively male membership had been highlighted by the accession of Elizabeth II in 1952. Consequently the Life Peerages Act, 1958, permitted the creation of women life peers, but excluded women who were peers in their own right. This was only rectified in 1963.

By 1968, women had undoubtedly attained a more prominent profile within politics. Those who gained office often became well-recognised public figures. They had proven that their political skills were wide-ranging to the extent that they were no longer associated so overwhelmingly with women's issues. Yet women MPs were still criticised for their reticence in debates and apparent unwillingness to push themselves forward. The all-pervading public school atmosphere of the House of Common certainly acted as a deterrent as did the perception that men took greater interest in female MPs' dress than their politics. Finally, the pitifully low numbers of women reaching Parliament provided the starkest evidence that political equality was as elusive as social and economic equality.

8 Conclusion

> **KEY ISSUE** What had women achieved by 1968?

In 1945, feminism in Britain lost its momentum, faced with a resumption of conservative values regarding women's role in society. Underlying attitudes towards women resurfaced, demonstrating that the war had been but a temporary respite during which women had tasted greater social and economic emancipation. Nevertheless, the emphasis after 1945 on promoting domestic roles for women, as witnessed in employment, education and the Welfare State, did not suppress entirely the desire for a more independent status amongst women. Most significantly, as the country emerged from the years of economic austerity, women realised that they could be not only generators of the growing national prosperity, namely as workers in the new light industries, but also beneficiaries of that prosperity. One of the most important changes for women, therefore, was to regard work less as an economic life-line, supplementing basic family wages, and more as a means of improving and enhancing family life. With more disposable income, women could envisage greater personal independence. In conjunction with increased educational opportunities, it also became more desirable to pursue a worthwhile career.

The realisation that women could direct their lives themselves rather than conform to male expectations of their allotted place in society gained further impetus during the 60s, spurred on by a proliferation of challenges to the status quo. Whether the medium was CND, music, drugs or easier contraception, there was an abiding sense that emancipation was viable in many forms. Most significantly, the generation of feminists emerging in the late 60s were less preoccupied with the traditional themes of the women's movement – equal pay and equal rights – and more focused on sexual freedoms and abortion rights. Supported by numerous feminist publications, women started to question whether they could achieve their goals through collaboration with men. The fiftieth anniversary of women's suffrage in 1968 was an occasion for re-evaluation of what women had achieved. For many women, it illustrated the historic failure of feminism to address the real causes of women's oppression. As Chapter 7 will discuss, the symbolic significance of 1968 was just one of several catalysts which inspired the Women's Liberation Movement of the 1970s.

References

1 Penny Summerfield, 'Women, War and Social Change: Women in Britain in World War II', in Arthur Marwick, ed., *Total War and Social Change* (Macmillan, 1988), p. 98.
2 Viola Klein, *Britain's Married Women Workers* (Routledge and Kegan Paul, 1965), p. 33.
3 *Ibid.*, p. 35.
4 Nancy Sear, 'The World of Work', in The Six Point Group, *In Her Own Right* (George G. Harrap and Co. Ltd., 1968), pp. 47–8.
5 *Ibid.*, p. 46.
6 Elizabeth Roberts, *Women and Families: An Oral History, 1940–1970* (Blackwell, 1995), pp. 57–8.
7 Alva Myrdal and Viola Klein, *Women's Two Roles, Home and Work* (Routledge and Kegan Paul, 1956), p. 142.
8 Klein, *Britain's Married Workers*, p. 48.
9 John Newsom, *The Education of Girls* (Faber and Faber Ltd., 1948), p. 12.
10 *Ibid.*, pp. 110–11.
11 Cited in April Carter, *The Politics of Women's Rights* (Longman, 1988), p. 38.
12 'The Education and Training of Girls: A Study by the Women's Group on Public Welfare' (National Council of Social Service, 1962), p. 113.
13 Cited in Elizabeth Wilson, *Only Halfway to Paradise: Women in Postwar Britain: 1945–1968* (Tavistock Publications, 1980), p. 72.

14 Cited in Ann Shearer, *Woman: Her Changing Image* (Thorsons Publishing Group, 1987), p. 52.
15 Sara Maitland, ed., *Very Heaven: Looking Back at the 1960s* (Virago Press, 1988), p. 151.
16 Betty Friedan, *The Feminine Mystique* (Penguin Books, 1965), p. 299.

Summary Diagram
Post-war Britain, 1945–68: a New Era

POST-WAR TRENDS AND DEVELOPMENTS		
ECONOMIC	**THE WELFARE STATE**	**THE FAMILY**
– Post-war labour shortages – Largest occupation groups – factory & domestic workers – Women encouraged to do 'feminine' work – Equal pay introduced in Civil Service, teaching & local government	– 1946 – National Insurance Act & National Health Service Act – Introduction of family allowances, maternity benefit, free universal health care	– New trends in child care – Families more socially insular – Family planning more widely available – Increase in divorce rate
EDUCATION	**CAMPAIGNS BY WOMEN**	**ROLE IN POLITICS**
– 1944 – Education Act – Secondary Education for all 11–15 year olds – Curriculum still gender-biased – 1960s – expansion of higher education	– Equal pay – CND – 1967 Abortion Act	– Women still deterred from entering politics – Assumption that women MPs were more expert in 'women's issues' – Promotion of women in Harold Wilson's Cabinet

Working on Chapter 6

From the notes you have made on this chapter and those of previous chapters, you should now be acquiring a fairly sound understanding of the various factors that affected the nature of women's lives in Britain. A first test of that understanding is to make sure that you can tackle the questions raised in the Key Issues in this chapter. Make brief notes on each section, making sure that you have addressed both concepts of causation and consequence.

Your second test is to consider how these different influences interacted and affected each other. For example, women's attitudes regarding their status within the family were affected by legislation, but what were the influences helping to shape legislation? Were more women working because of a shortage in manpower, or because work gave welcome release from domestic routines? How do these factors connect? A 'mind map' on which different ideas are noted, with arrows showing the links between issues would be one way to form an overall picture of what is a fairly complex pattern of cause and effect. Finally, write down what you think were the most important developments for women between 1945 and 1968, making sure that you understand why they happened.

Source-based questions on Chapter 6

1. Women's Ambitions
Read the following extracts: Elizabeth Roberts on page 102, Viola Klein on page 103, John Newsom on pages 105–6 and the 1962 Working Party on Education, page 107. Answer the following questions.

a) What did Newsom think about the 'pioneers of a higher education'? Why did he hold this opinion? (*2 marks; 3 marks*)

b) To what extent do the other sources agree or disagree with Roberts' conclusions regarding women's ambitions for themselves? (*6 marks*)

c) In what ways do the arguments presented by the 1962 Working Party differ from those put forward by Newsom? (*6 marks*)

d) How useful are these sources in explaining girls' improvements in education between 1945 and 1968? (*8 marks*)

e) Using the sources and your own knowledge, how far were educational policies responsible for women's low expectations of themselves after the war? (*10 marks*)

Hints and advice: Question 1a) tests your comprehension of the source. Clearly your ability to provide a good answer will depend on how well you have understood the background in which Newsom was writing and his aims in producing his report. With Question 1c) aim to make the comparisons point by point rather than dealing first with one and then the other source. With Question 1d) you not only need to evaluate each source but also indicate an awareness of other information which might be relevant to the question. Finally, 1e) uses the sources as a stimulus so that, in conjunction with your own knowledge, you can develop a more extended 'essay' type answer.

Answering essay questions on chapter 6

1. To what extent did economic opportunities for women expand between 1945 and 1968?

2. 'Between 1945 and 1968, women's lives were directed by conservative values'. Do you agree?

7 The Modern Age, 1968–2000

POINTS TO CONSIDER

This chapter analyses the impact of the Women's Liberation Movement and the subsequent developments which affected the status of women in Britain during the last decades of the twentieth century. During your initial reading, you should identify the main characteristics and aims of the Women's Liberation Movement, and then note the main social and economic advances which affected women during this period. Try to establish some understanding of the relative importance of other key influences, such as government intervention and changes in public attitudes.

KEY DATES

1968		Ford Dagenham strike.
		National Joint Action Committee for Women's Rights (NJACWR) founded.
1969	**May**	NJCACWR rally in Trafalgar Square.
1970	**Feb**	First National Women's Liberation Conference, Ruskin College Oxford.
		Equal Pay Act.
1973		Brixton Black Women's Group established.
1975		'Wages for Housework' campaign.
	Mar	National Women's Aid Federation founded.
		Sex Discrimination Act.
		Employment Protection Act.
		National Abortion Campaign launched.
1978		Organisation of Women of Asian and African Descent founded.
1979		Margaret Thatcher became first British female Prime Minister.
1980		Employment Act.
1981	**Aug**	'Women for Life on Earth' march to Greenham Common.
1986		Sex Discrimination Act.
1993		Labour Party decision to promote selection of female parliamentary candidates.
1997		New Labour government: 120 women MPs elected.

1 Introduction

> **KEY ISSUE** What were the distinctive features of the women's movement after 1968?

The political and cultural radicalism of the 1960s proved to be the precursor to the emergence of a dynamic, challenging feminist movement in Britain in 1970. Student protests against authority, such as those concerning American intervention in Vietnam or the left-wing student riots in Paris in 1968, created a new climate of militancy and lack of deference to the status quo. Against this background, the women's movement gained fresh inspiration, acquiring both a new-found confidence and ideology.

As discussed in Chapter 6, new feminist literature facilitated the emergence of a women's movement which was to be quite distinct from previous forms of feminism. Women's consciousness was raised by authors who developed new critiques and analyses of women's status within society. These ideas generated fresh determination to re-examine and re-evaluate women's lack of rights in all aspects of their lives. Several key events then helped to instigate what proved to be a major causal factor in bringing about reforms for women.

The critical reappraisal of women's position in society, the causes of oppression and the potential solutions propounded were all direct results of the new outspoken feminism. Yet what is also notable is that the generation of fresh ideas did provoke reactions beyond those directly involved in the movement. In conjunction with women's own efforts to change their lives there was also a greater readiness by both government and society as a whole to address key issues of inequality. As a result, significant new legislation was passed, such as the Equal Pay Act of 1970 and the Sex Discrimination Act, 1975.

But despite what appeared to be major advances in terms of social and economic reforms, the momentum of the 1970s faltered within a decade. This was prompted by the effects of increasing divergence within the feminist movement and less sympathetic government policies instigated by Margaret Thatcher. Consequently, the chance to sustain a rapid process of change was lost. Although opportunities for women had greatly expanded and there was far wider acceptance for the need for equality, these restraints on women's progress inevitably hindered the consolidation of equal rights.

2 The Women's Liberation Movement

> **KEY ISSUES** How and why did the Women's Liberation
> Movement develop in Britain? What were the main objective of
> the movement? What were the reasons for ideological divisions
> within it?

a) Background

During the 1960s women had gained what they perceived to be
greater sexual freedom, helped undoubtedly by the introduction of
the contraceptive pill. Increasingly, though, feminists questioned
whether control over reproduction merely aggravated the likelihood
that men would regard women as sexual objects. Many women
involved in the left-wing student protest movements of the late 1960s
felt themselves excluded from decision-making by radical male students who saw it as their male prerogative to change world politics.
Where was the equality in this new world if the sexist view of women
as pretty objects but with little brain to make important decisions still
underlay male thinking?

One of the instigators of change came unexpectedly from women
factory workers at Ford's Dagenham car plant rather than from ideological, middle-class feminists. In 1968, 300 sewing machinists at the
plant went on strike demanding that their jobs be upgraded and re-
evaluated from unskilled to semi-skilled status, a move which would
then accord them pay rates on a par with men doing similar types of
jobs. Further kudos was accorded to the trade union protest when the
Employment Secretary, Barbara Castle, invited the striking women to
tea. The three-week strike provoked Ford into agreeing to the principle of equal pay and to investigating ways of preventing future discrimination against women. Although the machinists remained
classified as unskilled workers and were only granted 95 per cent of
men's pay, they had nevertheless gained an important victory in terms
of women's working rights.

Previous trade union support for equal pay had been somewhat
half-hearted, but the Dagenham protest, followed by similar strikes in
London, Hull and, in 1969, Manchester and Coventry, created a
forum of opinion which recognised that trade unionism should be
more interventionist in upholding women's rights. In 1968, the
National Joint Action Committee for Women's Rights (NJACWR) was
founded, adopting a five-point charter which called for TUC support
for equal rights. The following May, the organisation held an important rally in Trafalgar Square which was endorsed by the Labour movement. These developments ensured that women's liberation in
Britain would be closely associated with class politics, with both its
language and ideology reflecting the radicalism of left-wing ideas.

The final catalyst for women's liberation occurred when a group of women led by Sheila Rowbotham held a separate workshop for female historians at Ruskin College Oxford in February 1970. Initially only anticipating an attendance of about 300, in fact the First National Women's Liberation Conference attracted nearly 600 women. As the participants explored the issues that were relevant to women, there emerged a strong consensus and real sense of mission regarding future aims of the women's movement. Four key objectives were agreed: equal pay, equal education and opportunity, 24-hour nurseries and finally free contraception and abortion on demand. A Women's National Coordinating Committee was also established to act as an umbrella organisation for local women's groups.

b) The Nature of the Women's Liberation Movement in Britain

By the end of 1970, a host of different women's organisations had been founded across the country. One of their distinguishing features was the fact that they were very decentralised and autonomous. Although they were all inspired by a strong desire to address the oppression of women, each group often focused on a local specific campaign. One such cause was the plight of women night cleaners in London. At least 90 per cent of all cleaning jobs were done by women, who were often immigrants receiving as little as £18 a week. Feminists attacked the exploitation of this cheap source of labour. Another campaign was fought within the Post Office where, although the principle of equal pay had been established, equal rights were still denied. As one female post office worker claimed,

1 We did equal work but we didn't have equal rights. We received less
  sick pay for one thing. The women only got it for three months,
  whereas the men got full pay for six months. There were no promotion
  rights ... Not one of us could go to the first rung of the ladder, to
5 Postman Higher Grade.[1]

The campaigns for equal pay and equal rights formed the cornerstone of feminist activism during the 1970s. But correlated with these objectives was the recognition that women's chances of equality would only advance if sexual divisions and gender stereotyping within society were eroded. Thus two key grievances were the status of women within the family and the lack of educational opportunities for girls.

Although schools had begun in the 1960s to address curriculum problems and the underachievement of girls in education, the feminist movement of the 1970s argued that persistent gender bias in schools was undermining any potential for long-term improvement. Feminist analysis of literature, such as the survey conducted by the feminist magazine *Shrew* in October 1973, led to a critical examination of how textbooks portrayed the different sexes. Invariably a science illustration showed an experiment being conducted by a boy whilst a girl was a passive onlooker. History books focused on the achievements of men, with regular references to individuals, whilst women were mentioned only in general terms. Teachers, when questioned, admitted that a higher percentage of their attention was afforded to boys. Furthermore, the assumption that girls should gain qualifications in domestic science and needlework, rather than woodwork, and that girls were more able at biology than physics or chemistry was still very prevalent. In exams, boys outperformed girls with the result that more boys entered higher education and trained for a professional career. In 1970/71, 241,000 men were in full-time higher education compared to 173,000 women.[2] In 1974/75, women constituted only ten per cent of all solicitors and seven per cent of doctors.[3]

It was the persistent efforts of the women's liberation movement which helped to raise awareness within the educational profession of the extent to which sexism was still endemic. Many teachers were just unconscious of how much they discriminated against girls. Feminists campaigned through workshops, conferences and surveys to publicise the sexist treatment of girls as well as to encourage reforms. Their priority was to demonstrate that unless social values were changed, starting with the education system, 'masculine' and 'feminine' ideologies would continue to promote a gender segregated world of employment and educational opportunities. The efforts of the Women's Liberation Movement undoubtedly helped to influence the climate of opinion. In the early 1980s the Inner London Education Authority (ILEA) adopted a number of measures to tackle approaches to girls' education, including an Equal Opportunities Unit which established projects in school. As Frances Morrell, leader of ILEA, acknowledged in 1985, the commitment of feminists to equal opportunities had been crucial in influencing ILEA's policies:

1 The Authority owes a great debt to their persistence, imagination and commitment. Their collective pressure over the years has undoubtedly succeeded in shifting the official perception of sex equality from a fringe element within education to part of the definition of mainstream good
5 educational practice ... [4]

The second area where women faced consistent stereotyping was their status within the family. Through discussions in conscious-raising groups across the country, women questioned their 'domestic destiny'. The ties of marriage and children meant that women could not establish their own independent identity. Moreover, they remained a cheap source of labour, which was totally expendable according to prevailing economic conditions. Campaigns such as 24-hour nurseries were fought in order to facilitate women's employment prospects and eliminate the causes of oppression. Without adequate childcare facilities, women were forced to remain in domestic roles, denied financial independence and social status. Across the country, therefore, women set up play-groups, agitated for more nurseries, and sought the involvement of men in childcare in order to break the cycle of entrenched domesticity.

There was, however, a recognition that some women preferred not to work. The 'Wages for Housework' campaign argued that house-work had as much value as other work and should be recompensed accordingly. Another prominent campaign was to offer protection for women suffering from violence within the home. In March 1975, the National Women's Aid Federation (NWAF) was founded in order to provide temporary refuges for women and children suffering from mental or physical harassment. Around 100 Women's Aid groups affil-iated to the NWAF and between them they ran about 150 refuges in England and Wales, offering support, advice and protection for bat-tered women. The achievement of the NWAF was to bring into the public domain a sensitive and often suppressed fact of family life, namely that women were frequently the silent victims of male violence.

Many of the ideas inspiring the Women's Liberation Movement focused on granting women autonomy within their lives as well as seek-ing structural changes within a gender divided society. One key area in which women sought greater control was in healthcare, where tra-ditionally a male-dominated medical profession had shown little empa-thy for the health issues that troubled women. Self-help health centres developed in conjunction with a proliferation of literature which enabled women to discover and share information about women's health and which offered appropriate advice. One of the eventual out-comes of these developments was greater choice in childbirth methods.

Other reforms sought were free contraception and abortion on demand. The right to an abortion, albeit limited by the legislation of the 1967 Abortion Act, came under threat from anti-abortionists such as the Society for the Protection of Unborn Children (SPUC) who sought to get the Abortion Act either repealed or modified. Feminists rallied to defend what they considered to be a vital right, namely the entitlement to conclude an unwanted pregnancy. Although not all feminists agreed with abortion, this was a cause that aroused heated passions amongst many women. Consequently, the National Abortion Campaign (NAC) was founded, bringing together feminist organis-ations throughout the country. The network of groups affiliating to the NAC typified the nature of the women's movement in Britain. Single issues would unite women into a powerful pressure group, but each local organisation would still retain its own agenda for defeating other causes of women's oppression.

c) Feminist Dissension

In the early days of the Women's Liberation Movement, women were brimming with zealous enthusiasm as they collectively explored the causes of women's oppression and developed radical theories with which to revolutionise society. But the very political nature of the movement exposed it to in-fighting, differences of interpretation, and clashes of ideology. As a result, the movement was weakened by both the lack of cohesion and any co-ordinated national campaign. The main groups were:

- **socialist feminists** derived their ideas from Marx's theory of class conflict. They identified capitalism as the main source of women's oppression. Women had been relegated to a position of subservience by a predominantly male workforce. Women were expected to manage the family, provide cheap labour whilst men were main breadwinners. The State, therefore, had to assume greater responsibility for childcare and the elderly so that women could become proper wage-earners. They were prepared to work alongside men.

- **radical feminists** attacked the system of patriarchy whereby men dominated women within the family. They advocated freedom from men and female autonomy. This entailed a rejection of heterosexual relationships in favour of lesbianism.

- **Brixton Black Group (1973) & Organisation of Women of Asian and African Descent (1978).** Both groups defended interests of Black and Asian women. Concerned about racial discrimination and immigration policies which broke up family units. Campaigned for communal facilities – childcare and laundry – so that more women could work and support their families.

By the 1980s, dissension within the women's movement in Britain had forced many women to accept that their early visions of securing liberation would have to be modified. Too often, there was disagreement about methodology, whether to co-operate with the Labour movement, to collaborate with men or not. Moreover, the focus of protest tended to shift as exemplified by the emergence of the protests at Greenham Common.

The Campaign for Nuclear Disarmament had continued to attract feminists who saw the peace campaign as a means of rejecting male violence. But protest activity was fairly muted during the 1970s, weakened by the many disparate views within feminism. The event which galvanised women into action was the decision to base Cruise and Pershing II nuclear missiles at the RAF base at Greenham Common in Berkshire which had become the base for the US Airforce (USAF). The first protest was led by Ann Pettitt who headed a march of 36 women, four men and a few children from Cardiff to Greenham Common in August 1981. The 'Women for Life on Earth' walked 120 miles and as they approached the airbase, decided to replicate the actions of the suffragettes by chaining themselves to the perimeter railings. It was an action which caught the attention of the media as well as other peace protesters. Having gained publicity, however, they realised that the protest would have to be sustained. A permanent camp was established at the base, with satellite camps developing elsewhere along the nine-mile perimeter fence. Conditions were often appalling especially during the cold winter. What was so remarkable about the consequent protests at Greenham was the fact that women with no previous experience of involvement in feminism were drawn into this exceptional peace movement. Inevitably the camp attracted seasoned campaigners, but it also involved grandmothers, women with jobs who would visit for just a few days, young women experiencing their first taste of activism.

Not all women were comfortable with this new direction within feminism. There were criticisms from those who feared that the socialist aims of the movement had been supplanted by a set of ideas which extolled maternalism; in one rally on 12 December 1982, 30,000 women gathered round the base, pinning baby clothes to the perimeter fence. This peace movement seemed to emphasise connections between peace, security of the family, rights of mothers to reject violence; it left socialists uneasy that the fight against capitalism was being sidelined. Nevertheless, despite internal arguments and the many battles with the authorities over incursions into the base, the Greenham Common protest remained a prominent focal point for the feminist movement during the 1980s. In March 1991, the last of the cruise missiles were removed from Greenham Common in response to the ending of the Cold War. To the women protesters, however, this seemed a vindication of their resistance.

3 State Initiatives and Public Policy

> **KEY ISSUE** What role did government play in advancing the cause of women after 1968?

Despite the dissension and diversity of aims within the Women's Liberation Movement, one significant outcome was to render women more assertive and confident. Although many people outside the movement reacted negatively to the images of women campaigning for issues like free abortions, others gradually accepted the premise that social and economic reforms were required. There emerged, therefore, a climate of opinion which was more receptive to new initiatives. This in turn affected government thinking. In 1970 the effects of lobbying by the women's movement, combined with support from the Labour movement and the presence of a Labour government committed to reform, resulted in the first of several landmark pieces of legislation which marked a turning point for women.

Some of that legislation is outlined in the table on page 130.

Key Legislation

Equal Pay Act 1970
As from December 1975 women were entitled to receive equal pay if 'employed in work which is the same as, or broadly similar to, that of a man; or in a job which, although different from that of a man, has been given an equal value under a job evaluation scheme'.[5] Sick pay, holiday entitlements and bonuses were also affected.

Employment Protection Act 1975
This gave important rights to working women who were expecting a baby. Women with two years' service with their employers were entitled to six weeks' paid maternity leave and to return to their job up to 29 weeks after the birth. The Act excluded part-time women working fewer than 16 hours a week unless they had worked for five years with an employer. Women could not be dismissed because they were pregnant.

Sex Discrimination Act 1975
It was illegal to discriminate against women in the areas of employment and training, education, housing, and the provision of goods, services and facilities. Two types of discrimination were defined. Direct discrimination applied to any case where a person was treated less favourably on grounds of their sex. Indirect discrimination concerned the application of a set of conditions, such as in a job requirement, which in practice favoured one sex. It was also illegal to treat a married woman less favourably than a single person, such as when considering eligibility for a mortgage. The Act set up the Equal Opportunities Commission to oversee both the implementation of the Equal Pay Act and the SDA, and to arbitrate in cases of discrimination.

Social Security Pensions Act 1975
A major reform for women which granted equal access to occupational pension schemes. Women who had ceased working due to family commitments received a state pension provided they had been employed and paid full insurance contributions for 20 years. From 1978 married women were entitled to the same employment and sickness benefits as men.

Domestic Violence and Matrimonial Proceedings Act 1976
This Act was passed as a result of lobbying by the NWAF and the persistence of Jo Richardson, M.P. It allowed a woman, either as a wife or living with a man as his wife, to apply for court injunction to protect them (and their children) from a violent partner. Previously an injunction could only be obtained if other legal proceedings such as divorce were instigated. But the law gave no protection from an ex-husband.

Employment Protection Act 1977
This extended the employment rights of full-time workers to all those working a 16 hour week, or eight hours if in the same job for five years.

Employment Act 1980
Introduced by a Conservative government, this Act exempted small firms employing fewer than six people from granting women the right to return to their job after having a baby.

Sex Discrimination Act 1986
The British government was forced to comply with European Community directives on equal treatment for men and women. Much of the remaining conditions under which discrimination had continued after 1975 were now declared illegal.

Two acts which were of great symbolic importance to women were the Equal Pay Act 1970 and the Sex Discrimination Act 1975. Equal pay had long formed the crux of women's campaigns, but it was not until 1970 that the political commitment to reform manifested itself. Since the war, although the numbers of women in employment had risen, they were invariably concentrated in the lowest paid jobs such as catering, hairdressing and retail. 98 per cent of all typists were women. The effect of increased employment for women, however, had led to greater pay differentials between men and women's wages. By 1970 women's average weekly earnings as a percentage of men's had declined by nine per cent since 1950.

Why was equal pay introduced in 1970? First, a precedent was established when equal pay was accorded to white-collar workers in the public services such as civil servants and teachers. Second, the activity of women trade unionists, as illustrated by the Ford Dagenham strike, heightened awareness of the injustice of pay differentials. Third, a 1964 Labour election pledge to implement equal pay had increased expectations which, although unrealised during the 1964–66 Labour government, led to intense lobbying during the ensuing Labour administration, 1966–70. Fourth, in 1968 Harold Wilson had appointed Barbara Castle as Secretary of State for Employment. It was Barbara Castle's genuine sympathy to the principle of equal pay and to improving the rights of working-class women at work, plus her energy and determination to seek compromises both with the TUC and the Confederation of British Industry and to pilot a bill through parliament, which resulted in one of the key legislative initiatives for women's rights in the post-war era. It would not have been possible, however, without the co-operation of the Labour government, heightened pressures from the women's movement and the general climate of the age, which made most men realise the injustice women were suffering. Slowly but gradually, women's pay began to increase, although as the table below illustrates, legislation alone was not sufficient to rectify inequalities.

Women's average gross earnings

(excluding the effects of overtime) as a percentage of men's, 1970–84.[6]

1970	1975	1980	1981	1982	1983	1984
63.1	72.1	73.5	74.8	73.9	74.2	73.5

The second notable piece of legislation to affect women's status was the 1975 Sex Discrimination Act. As with equal pay, the issue of discrimination against women had formed the basis of consistent lobbying by feminists for many years, but had gained fresh momentum with the onset of the Women's Liberation Movement. Intense pressure by numerous women's groups, including the Fawcett Society and the Six Point Group, had accompanied two attempts, first by Joyce Butler, M.P, and then Willie Hamilton, M.P, to bring in a Private Member's Bill to end discrimination. Neither bill succeeded, and so it was the Labour government elected in 1974 which subsequently spearheaded the Sex Discrimination Act. In principle, the act was a significant reform as it encapsulated in law the right for women to be treated equally with men. Yet it was riddled with loopholes. For instance, a woman had to prove that she was the victim of discrimination, but if the relevant documents were withheld, that task was extremely difficult. Nevertheless, the enactment of legislation, in conjunction with changing social attitudes, was an essential prerequisite to securing further equality for women.

Other legislation during the 1970s and 1980s (see pages 130–1) maintained the gradual process of securing women's rights in terms of employment, welfare benefits, pay and their status within the family. Yet despite the promotion of women's interests, together with more emancipated attitudes towards the role of women in society, and the added impetus of a very pro-active women's movement, it was clear by the 1980s that women were far from attaining the goals so proudly proclaimed in 1970.

4 The End of the Twentieth Century

> **KEY ISSUES** What were the distinctive features defining the status of women in Britain at the end of the twentieth century? To what extent have the objectives of the Women's Liberation Movement been sustained?

These two issues are closely interrelated as it is against the original aims of the 1970s Women's Liberation Movement that the subsequent progress of women can best be judged. If emancipation, both economic and social, formed the basic objectives of feminists, then to what extent was that realised by the end of the century and what were the reasons, if any, for perhaps only limited success?

One key factor affecting the pace of reforms for women was Margaret Thatcher's election as Conservative Prime Minister in 1979. Although it was undoubtedly a major achievement to become Britain's first female Prime Minister, Margaret Thatcher did little to serve the interests of her sex. Liberal reforms of the 1970s were supplanted by an emphasis on free markets, deregulation, and the reduction in state protection for vulnerable sections of society. Policies such as those advocated by the Family Policy Group in 1983 reduced the role of the state by shifting the responsibility for care of the sick and the elderly towards private individuals and, most probably, women.

The underlying philosophy of Thatcher's Conservatism was well exemplified by the comment made by one of her senior ministers, Patrick Jenkin, in 1979:

> If the good Lord had intended us all having equal rights to go out to work and to behave equally, you know he really wouldn't have created man and woman.[7]

Under Margaret Thatcher many of the advances previously made by women were curtailed as the government attempted to revive women's role within the family. However, government policies were not solely responsible for developments after 1980. Much of the fervour of the earlier liberation movement diminished as the reality of many women's projects, such as shared parenting, proved difficult to realise in practice. As Sheila Rowbotham admitted, women might have gained freedom through changes in the upbringing of children, but this often entailed a loss of power and status at home without the compensation of enhanced status at work. Many women, therefore, reacted against the pressure to return to work, claiming that motherhood was as valid an occupation as any other. Finally, there was considerable evidence that whereas gender segregation at work was breaking during the mid-1970s, this trend was being reversed by 1979. One analysis of women's employment record noted, 'the total position of women at work in terms of pay, conditions and security of employment deteriorated sharply in the 1980s'.[8]

a) The Economic Position of Women

The policies of the Conservative Party under Margaret Thatcher and her successor, John Major, had a number of implications for women's economic status in Britain. One key issue was the failure to address the continuing inequalities between men's and women's pay. Despite the Equal Pay Act, four million women were still on low pay. In 1970 women's average hourly wage was 63 per cent of men's wages; by 1999 it was only 80 per cent. For part-time workers the differential was much greater, 59 per cent. Men earned larger salaries because they usually worked longer hours. Only at a professional level did women's wages begin to match those of their male counterparts.

In 1997 the Labour Party was elected to government for the first time in 18 years. Since then, government policies have demonstrated a more positive approach to the problems of low pay for women. The introduction of the minimum wage in April 1999 is considered to have had a notable effect in narrowing the gender pay gap. Hairdressers, for example, received an average pay rise of 11.7 per cent, giving them a new hourly rate of £4.64 an hour, higher than the new minimum wage. Others to benefit were waitresses and petrol pump attendants. But pay disparity still prevails despite legislation. One report in *The Guardian* on 11 November 1999 revealed that Sue MacGregor, one of the main presenters of BBC Radio 4's *Today* programme, received £20,000 less per year than her male colleagues, John Humphreys and James Naughtie.

Throughout the last 30 years of the twentieth century there was a steady increase in the participation of women in the labour market. In 1984, 30 per cent of all full-time workers were women, whereas by 1995 it was 32.7 per cent. Amongst part-time workers, women formed 82 per cent of the workforce.[9] Yet by far the highest number still worked in lower grades of the service sectors – clerical, secretarial, nursing, sales assistants, health professionals. Men continued to dominate managerial levels. According to the Institute of Management, only 9.6 per cent of all directors were women in 2000.[10] In the professions, women have made some significant advances, law and accountancy being two notable examples, whilst within the Civil Service the number of women in top posts increased from four per cent in 1984 to ten per cent by 1994. Appointments within the public sector have clearly reflected a very positive concern to redress gender imbalance; selection procedures were adjusted so that women were included on shortlists, although selection on merit remained the criteria for appointments. Indeed, critics would argue that the bias in favour of men is still much in evidence and has not been eradicated, despite initiatives like *Opportunity 2000*. This was launched by employers in 1991 and was a scheme whereby participants agreed to subscribe to a number of specific goals such as job-sharing and paternity leave. But the fact that many men still hesitate to take paternity leave suggests that women are more likely to be the ones taking longer career breaks, with the inevitable result that they fail to narrow the gender gap in relation to both jobs and pay.

b) The Social Status of Women

One of the most dramatic developments for women over the last 20 years has been the changing face of family life. This is demonstrated by the sharp increase in the number of women either delaying or even opting out of having children (see table below). Whereas most women used to commence their families in their twenties, fertility rates for women aged 35–39 have nearly doubled over the last two decades as have figures for the number of women aged 40 who are still childless.

	1976	1998
Aged 20–29	69	48
Aged 30–39	20	42

Fertility rates (percentage of live births) for women aged in their twenties and in their thirties[11]

Other significant trends have been the reduction in the number of married couples with the proportion of women under the age of 50 who were married declining from two-thirds to one half since the mid-1980s. Correspondingly, there has been a much higher tendency for women to cohabit, perhaps only getting married when they start a family.

Why should these new patterns of family life have evolved only late in the twentieth century? One obvious factor is that fewer women have felt inclined to curtail career prospects purely for marriage and children. At the same time, however, women experience contradictory pressures in that they are torn between work and family. Indeed many women sense that in order to gain any measure of equality, they have to compete with men on men's terms. The concessions to women have not been sufficient to reduce women's dual burden of work and family. Government initiatives to expand nursery care, especially since 1997, are taking effect, but many women still have to resort to private childcare arrangements if they want to work. One significant change, for example, has been the way in which the domestic service market has been stimulated by women's needs for nannies, cleaners and gardeners. In sharp contrast to the pre-war domestic servant, well-qualified nannies can expect salaries in London of maybe £320 a week, plus a car and even, if they live-in, a flat. But for women unable to afford such luxuries, the burden of housework seems to be as acute as ever, despite a growing band of 'house-husbands'. Commenting in *Social Trends 30*, which looked at how the country had changed since 1970, the historian A.H. Halsey noted:

1 Despite many advances, the life of women has not become unequivocally more leisured. Hours of paid employment have been shortened and domestic chores eased by affluence; but sharing of domestic labour has moved glacially and at the end of the century remained in favour of
5 men. Women did 260 minutes a day of unpaid work, men 172.[12]

During the last years of the twentieth century women have acquired a wealth of additional rights and benefits. In terms of healthcare, access to free family planning is taken for granted. The 1967 Abortion Act was amended in 1990 to permit a time limit of 24 weeks for the majority of abortions. Financial support for women has widened considerably – social security benefits for women caring for the sick and elderly, family credit to low income families as well as increases in statutory maternity pay. As a result of the 1999 Welfare Reform and Pensions Act women who get divorced are entitled to bring forward to the date of divorce 50 per cent of their husband's pension funds rather than having to wait until the man reaches pensionable age.

Women's individual rights have also been significantly enhanced. In response to protests by women, special police units now handle rape cases with the result that the number of reported cases has increased. Some, at least, of the stigmatism attached to being a rape victim had been ameliorated. Another positive development was the Protection From Harassment Act, 1997, which, with its wide definition of harassment, enabled many women to gain restraining orders against men who persistently stalk them.

Undoubtedly, one of the most remarkable achievements over the last 20 years has been women's progress in education. The efforts to tackle the low expectations of girls have borne positive results in that now girls consistently outperform boys in examinations. At GCSE level, a higher percentage of girls gain A*–C grades, and whereas previously girls were surpassing boys in subjects such as English, foreign languages and history, they are now ahead in both mathematics and science. Since 1988/89 girls have outperformed boys at A Level with 24 per cent of girls and only 20 per cent of boys achieving two or more A Levels in 1998/99. This dramatic turn in educational standards amongst women has also had a major effect on the numbers attending higher education. Nearly five times as many women enrolled for higher education courses in 1998/99 (599,000) as in the early 1970s (173,000) whereas figures for men have only doubled (528,000 in 1998/99 compared to 241,000 in 1970/71).

Several factors explain these improvements. First, the determination to tackle sex stereotyping in schools, which was clearly encouraged by the activities of the Women's Liberation Movement, has had a very positive effect in promoting girls' self-confidence and raising expectations. Second, the introduction of the National Curriculum in England and Wales set universal standards of achievement, and in so doing ensured that equal opportunities were intrinsic to all subjects. The tendency of girls to study only biology as a science has been tackled by the fact that all three science subjects are prescribed by the National Curriculum as are all technology subjects. Third, there have been a number of initiatives to encourage girls and women to study science and technology and more enlightened careers advice has obviously been influential in shaping expectations of women. Fourth, the general climate of opinion towards women is significantly less gender biased, and so male attitudes have changed. This in itself has created conditions within which women feel more motivated to pursue a wider range of educational courses at all levels.

5 Conclusion

> **KEY ISSUE** Why were women unable to sustain the move for further emancipation?

During the 1970s, the radical and progressive ideas of the Women's Liberation Movement challenged many of society's accepted norms of behaviour. Not since the suffragettes had such a dynamic feminist movement succeeded in capturing the enthusiasm and involvement of so many women. The spontaneity with which local liberation organisations sprang up nationwide reflected widespread disaffection amongst women. Women were no longer prepared to seek reforms through co-operation with those in authority. This had only led to stagnation and compromise. What emerged during the 1970s was a fresh approach, one which was clearly directed by women on behalf of women.

As we study the last decades of the twentieth century, one abiding question remains. Why were women unable to sustain the momentum of the 1970s? The answer lies in understanding the complex range of factors that determine social and economic change. Undoubtedly, there were substantial achievements. The women's movement was a powerful force in breaking down traditional attitudes towards women. By publicising the extent to which gender bias and stereotyping still prevailed, women appealed to a general sense of injustice. Those in authority realised that the foundations on which such discrimination had been based in the past were no longer so tenable. Changing the climate of opinion was crucial in facilitating reforms.

But, in politics, legislative reform is formulated within the context of a party's overall philosophy. Throughout the twentieth century women have been dependent on whether the ruling party can perceive political advantage in pursuing women's issues. Since the 1970s, the thrust of reform has fluctuated significantly, as first Labour, then the Conservatives and finally Labour again defined their own approaches to policies affecting women. Without adequate representation in Parliament, women could do little to challenge the implementation of policies still largely determined by men.

The other key point to appreciate is that expectations amongst women are diverse and often contradictory. Not all women share the same goals, nor are the goals they seek always attainable. Some women are free to choose their particular life-style whether that is as a mother based at home or a career woman, but others are not. What is clear is that choices for women have expanded as the result of equal opportunity policies, but whether women have gained the right balance in their lives, most notably between work and family, remains an unresolved question. The differing status of women is further complicated by underlying social and economic conditions which inevitably leave some women more equal than others. It is these factors which will have to be addressed in the future if women are to overcome the discrimination that still prevails.

References

1 'Women Under Attack', Counter Information Services, p. 14.
2 'Social Trends 29' (Office for National Statistics, 1999), p. 60.
3 Sue Innes, *Making It Work: Women, Change and Challenge in the 1990s* (Chatto and Windus, 1995), p. 56.
4 Cited in Anna Coote and Beatrix Campbell, *Sweet Freedom: The Struggle for Women's Liberation* (Blackwell, 1987), pp. 200–201.
5 *Women in Britain*, (HMSO, 1996) p. 25.
6 Coote and Campbell, *Sweet Freedom*, p. 81.
7 Cited in Elizabeth Meeham, 'British Feminism from the 1960s to the 1980s', in Harold L. Smith, ed., *British Feminism in the Twentieth Century* (Edward Elgar, 1990), p. 202.
8 April Carter, *The Politics of Women's Rights* (Longman, 1988), p. 86.
9 *Women in Britain* p. 47
10 'National Management Salary Survey', Institute of Management/ Remuneration Economics, May 2000.
11 *The Guardian*, 21 June 2000, p. 7.
12 Cited in *The Daily Telegraph*, 27 January 2000, p. 3.

Summary Diagram
The Modern Age, 1968–2000

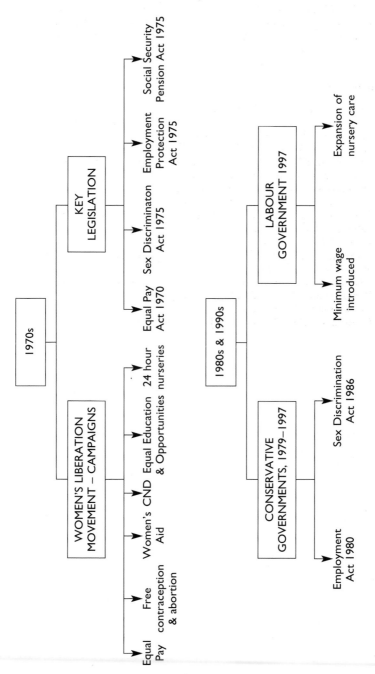

Working on Chapter 7

Having completed the chapter, you should now have outline notes on the main features and aims of the Women's Liberation Movement. You should also have a basic understanding of the economic, social and political status of women in Britain by the year 2000.

Returning to the Women's Liberation Movement, identify the main campaigns of the movement and try and evaluate what was so distinctive about these campaigns. When you work on your final overview, you will need to be able to compare and contrast the different stages of feminism during the twentieth century. Make sure you can explain why the momentum of the movement was lost.

Next, examine the legislative reforms and use the information to answer the key issue posed in Section 3. Then return to Section 4 so that you can build up a contextual understanding of women's position in Britain at the end of the century. Try a simple approach. What have women gained and what disadvantages do they still encounter?

Answering structured questions on Chapter 7

1. The Women's Liberation Movement

a) What was so distinctive about the Women's Liberation Movement of the 1970s compared with the preceding women's movement of the post-war period?

b) Why did support for the Women's Liberation Movement diminish by the mid-1980s?

c) How far was the Women's Liberation Movement responsible for changing attitudes towards women after 1970?

2. The Position of Women in Britain at the end of the Twentieth Century

a) 'Women's lives in Britain changed significantly between 1970 and 2000'. Discuss.

b) Why did women only achieve limited success in gaining greater equality with men after 1970?

Hints and advice: In Question 1, three types of questions are asked. 1a) is an analytical comparison which requires you to establish the key features of both movements and then to contrast the two. You might want to think about different aims and ideologies, methods, types of people involved and you will have to refer to material you read in Chapter 6 as well in order to write the essay. Comparative essays are usually more effective if you can deal with related points concerning both movements rather than discussing first one then the other in sequence. Question 1b) is a causation question where you have to look for different types of reasons for the decline in support. It will be important, for example, to think about internal and external factors as well as the range of causal factors within those categories. 1c) asks you to evaluate the extent to which the WLM was responsible for changing attitudes towards women. This is a question about judgement so in your plan you should set out key points which you think can be attributed to the WLM but then take a wider perspective and assess what other factors might be relevant in prompting change.

In Question 2 are both broader issues which test your understanding of the whole chapter. Be prepared to recognise that there may be no right answers to these questions as it is difficult to evaluate objectively such recent history.

8 Conclusion: Women 1900–2000

POINTS TO CONSIDER

The purpose of this chapter is to try to reach some overall understanding of how and why women's lives changed in Britain during the
twentieth century. As you read this chapter make short, clear notes
under two headings: major changes in women's lives and significance of
different forces affecting women's lives. By the end of the chapter, you
should have some picture of the relative importance of each issue discussed, and also how the range of causal factors interact.

1 An Overview of the Twentieth Century

KEY ISSUES Did women's lives improve substantially during the
twentieth century and what were the key factors which
influenced these developments?

In Chapter 1, two issues were addressed in order to create a framework within which an analysis of women's lives in Britain could evolve.
First, the status of women in Britain between 1900 and 1914 was examined so as to provide some criteria by which subsequent change could
be assessed. Otherwise it would be impossible to measure the *extent* of
change which affected women. The second issue concerned the influences which instigated that change. They were identified as follows:
the World Wars, political reform, economic and social progress, technological change, education, and philosophical ideas. During the
course of the book, there has been regular reference to these different factors because it is only by understanding the impact of these
forces that we can begin to appreciate the complex relationships
between *change* and *continuity*, *cause* and *effect* which brought about
advances, or indeed setbacks, in women's lives. It is, therefore, within
the context of these broad categories that our final evaluation of
women's changing role in twentieth-century Britain will be conducted.

a) The World Wars

The main issue to consider is whether the two World Wars instigated
or accelerated economic, social and political change for women. Was
emancipation, if that indeed occurred, only a short-term phenomenon or could it be argued that some aspects of women's lives were
changed permanently by the wars?

i) Women's Economic Status
Prior to the First World War, large numbers of working-class women

had worked in menial, largely unskilled jobs for very low wages. Their position in the workforce was overwhelmingly inferior to that of men, not least because the co-operation between employers and trade unionists ensured that skilled jobs were exclusive to men only. Thus women were frequently exploited for their cheap labour but, due to economic necessity, had little hope of rectifying these inequalities. Women had to accept an economic role in which their earnings were often an essential supplement to the family wage because men's wages were insufficient to support a family.

In both wars, women's labour became an essential component within the workforce with women undertaking numerous jobs previously regarded as 'men's work'. How did men and women respond to this dramatic development? The treatment of women's labour and attitudes towards women in the workplace were largely consistent during both wars. A common pattern was for jobs to be segregated according to gender, for skilled jobs to be 'diluted' so that women generally performed unskilled tasks for lower wages. These trends would appear to suggest that women's labour was perceived as merely a short-term solution to an exceptional problem and that underlying this approach was a determination to terminate any major female involvement in 'men's work' at the end of the wars.

But even if that may have been the intention of both government and employers, as exemplified by the large-scale dismissal of women from industry in 1918 and 1945, can women's economic contributions be so easily disregarded? One issue to consider is whether, in providing practical proof of their capabilities and skills, women acquired greater self-confidence and hence determination to improve their job opportunities. Although women continued to occupy mainly inferior positions within the labour market after the two wars, more women began to acquire professional qualifications. There was sufficient progress to ensure that women did not return to the economic status experienced prior to 1914. Obviously other factors also affected the changing nature of women's work, but it is important to appreciate that the two wars did widen opportunities for women. Expectations were raised, preconceived attitudes challenged.

ii) Social Change

To what extent did the two wars further social emancipation for women? There is ample evidence to support the assertion that women experienced a considerable degree of independence during the wars, that social conventions were relaxed and that women quickly learnt to assume new responsibilities especially within the family. But how permanent were these changes? At the conclusion of both wars, there was a concerted effort by governments to encourage women to resume their domestic roles. The welfare legislation of the inter-war years and the National Insurance and National Health Acts of 1946 all included underlying motives of seeking to enhance the attraction of domestic life. In many respects, these policies were successful in that large numbers of women endorsed the belief that their prime duty was to husband and children. However, if war did create opportunities for greater individual autonomy, how were these gains retained after 1945? Was there a connection between the relaxation of sexual mores during the wars, the acquisition of greater personal independence, and the growing desire of women after the wars to control their health, to have access to birth control and to have more shared responsibility within the family? Did the wars, at the very least, give some women the incentive to seek a more equitable status within society?

iii) Political Change

Although it is not easy to establish direct and immediate links between women's gradual economic and social emancipation and the two World Wars, there is a stronger case for suggesting that the limited franchise accorded to women in 1918 was in part a direct consequence of the First World War. The important point to consider is whether all the pre-conditions for extending the franchise to women were in place before the war and that such reform would have occurred regardless or whether the war did precipitate the process of reform. Only by revising Chapters 2 and 3 can you really establish some views on this question. Certainly the involvement of women in politics after 1918 was not dramatic. In contrast, the Second World War did offer women politicians a chance to acquire a more prominent political profile, but the question has to be asked as to why this was not sustained after 1945.

b) Political Reform

At the beginning of the century, women could only vote in local elections. Within 30 years they had full political equality with men, and women were already making a small but notable impact as MPs and members of government. Whereas it took nearly 90 years for complete male suffrage to be fully enacted (1832–1918), for women it took just ten years. That was in many respects a remarkable, although long overdue, achievement. But how do we measure women's subsequent involvement in politics? Why are the government and the House of Commons still dominated by men?

What has emerged during the many discussions on political change throughout the century is that whilst legislation created the potential for women to undertake more responsibility in government, it did not necessarily transform attitudes of both men and women towards supporting greater political involvement by women. Despite the fact that individual women have repeatedly gained respected political reputations, it has proved more difficult to shift entrenched opinions on the overall role that women should play in politics.

Clearly a number of factors explain women's hesitation to seek a political career – no long-term tradition of involvement in politics, lack of education, conflicts with family ties, low expectations of themselves. But though much of that had changed by the end of the century, still women remain under-represented in Parliament. In the general election of 1997, the highest number of women ever, 121, were successfully elected to Parliament, compared to 41 MPs in 1987. It might be argued that for one fifth of all MPs to be female was indeed a landmark achievement. But as the next election approached, it was evident that not so many women were prepared to stand for re-election. Furthermore, apart from the historic election of Margaret Thatcher as the first female prime minister, the extent to which other women have attained high office is somewhat limited. Although Tony Blair appointed five women to his cabinet, that number diminished during his first term of office.

In weighing up, therefore, just how successful women have been in politics since 1900, you might wish to evaluate the extent to which men have facilitated women's entry into politics. Although other institutions have endeavoured to counteract work practices that militate against women, the House of Commons shows little consideration to the needs of women MPs with families. Long parliamentary sittings are still an intrinsic part of life at Westminster. Moreover, what sort of impression of women MPs does it convey when, as in May 1997, the media hailed the 102 new female Labour MPs as 'Blair's Babes'?

c) Economic and Social Progress

What were the long-term trends in women's employment during the twentieth century and how important were these changes? As indicated above, women's economic status at the beginning of the century was one in which women were economically inferior to men. The female workforce was also very vulnerable, easy victims to fluctuating economic conditions. There were, however, several significant factors which had influenced changes in women's employment by 2000. First, domestic service ceased to be one of the prime sources of employment. This was partly accelerated by the First World War, but it was a trend that continued thereafter, despite government attempts to revive the attractions of domestic service. Second, the percentage of women working at home declined. Women sought work outside the home for reasons that were complex, but they reflected, among other things, a desire for greater economic independence and a chance to do something that was for themselves. However, the question remains as to why women continue to be employed primarily in the semi- or unskilled sectors, even when new industries have developed in Britain. Does women's willingness to do part-time work still ensure that certain gender barriers in employment prevail?

Another important development has been the expanding numbers of women gaining professional qualifications and working in jobs previously dominated by men. How has this been possible? The role of the women's movement in campaigning for wider employment opportunities was one key influence. Another factor was improved education which finally started to eradicate long-term discrimination against girls. Women's own expectations of what they can achieve have changed measurably over the century, but even more importantly, so have men's attitudes towards women. Finally, changing work pattern at all levels have been assisted by government legislation. Without a huge range of acts introducing concepts such as equal pay and equal opportunities, women would not have made so much progress.

In what other respects have women's lives been transformed during the twentieth century? During the first half of the century, most women would cease working after marriage in order to devote time to their family. But in the last 50 years, the balance between home and work has shifted, with implications not only for women's economic status but also for their position within the family. The recent effects of those changes were discussed mainly in Chapter 7. The question to consider, though, is how those changes came about. The role of legislation in improving women's welfare, health and legal rights was crucial because these reforms provided protection as well as reinforcing the view that inequalities were unacceptable. On the other hand, one might want to question why it was that such reforms were often enacted in rather piecemeal fashion for so much of the century.

As gender gaps have narrowed, so women have become far more assertive. Their self-confidence has not only been enhanced by the decline of sexual prejudice, but also by women's ability to compete with men on an equal footing. This has arisen not least because women can now determine if and when they should have children. It is worth just comparing again the sheer burden of childbearing that women endured at the beginning of the century with the freedom of choice available in 2000 in order to appreciate just how much women's lives changed during those hundred years.

d) Technological Change

In what ways has technological change in the twentieth century affected women? In terms of women's role in society outside the home the implications have been far-reaching. For example, developments in technology were clearly one factor in transforming the nature of women's jobs. The emergence of light industries provided new scope for women's employment, facilitating the move away from home-based work. However, there were perhaps some negative features to this trend in that the fairly repetitive, unskilled tasks associated with such industries perpetuated women's low status in the workforce. As technology has advanced – from typewriters to electric typewriters to computers – one issue to examine is whether this has resulted in largely positive or negative benefits for women.

Within the home, women's lives have been radically altered by the introduction of a wide range of consumer goods. Items such as tinned food in the 1950s, followed by frozen foods and ultimately ready-made meals, revolutionised the regime in the kitchen, as did the array of electrical goods which eased the burden of housework. On the one hand, the reduction of sheer physical work in the home was obviously welcome, but not all women saw the immediate advantages in having more free time. As the many magazines for women demonstrated, producing the 'perfect home' became a job in its own right, especially during the late 1940s and 1950s. Although many middle-class women had successfully escaped the confines of domesticity – assisted, it should be remembered, by paid female domestic help – it was not until feminist writers in the late 1960s challenged the concept of domestic happiness that more women begin to question the limited nature of their daily routines. Few women today would want to abandon the mass of gadgets available to the modern home, but given that surveys reveal that more women than men still do the housework, has technology really alleviated women's domestic responsibilities?

e) Education

The developments in education for women during the twentieth century were undoubtedly one of the major forces providing the momentum for change in women's lives. Lack of equal educational opportunities with men proved a severe handicap because, whilst some men at least were educated to assume leadership roles, women were taught only basic skills. Those gaining higher educational qualifications in the first few decades of the century were in a distinct minority. So how and why did educational provision for women change and what was the significance of those changes?

Government legislation was a prime factor behind the widening of educational opportunities for girls. As state provision of education expanded, girls were inevitable beneficiaries. They could no longer be sent out to work as soon as possible in order to supplement the family income. In theory, universal secondary education gave girls the chance to acquire the same qualifications as boys. But, as discussions in previous chapters have revealed, the curriculum was carefully controlled to ensure that girls retained a limited set of ambitions. In seeking the answers as to why the curriculum was designed to train girls for future motherhood, it is important to link up with other government polices aimed at women. So many of the economic and social reforms had as one of their objectives the promotion of women's domestic role. Education served as yet another useful tool by which girls' expectations could be carefully manipulated.

Once, however, it was accepted that equal opportunities had to be applied seriously to education, marked changes can be identified in how girls performed in schools and universities. Was legislation alone responsible for this progress? How much importance should be attributed to the impact of feminism on education? As with so many things that affected women's lives during the twentieth century, shifting attitudes and people's perceptions of women was as important as passing legislative reforms. The campaign, therefore, by feminists to remove all discrimination within schools on the basis of sex and their success in instilling women with greater self-confidence must surely have been a significant factor in encouraging women both to seek and take advantage of a more balanced and stretching curriculum. And as women have become more successful, so it has become harder to deny them the same opportunities as men.

f) Philosophy

The final factor which has been instrumental in transforming women's lives during the twentieth century has been the influence of feminist thought on both men and women. Campaigns for women's rights could not operate in a vacuum. Supporters of feminist issues, whether these were the suffrage, equal pay, welfare rights, equal opportunities, health or employment, had to be able to refer to a set of ideas or philosophies which provided the context in which they were campaigning. As we trace the development of these ideas during the course of the century, it is interesting to note how the fluctuating success of the feminist movement corresponded to the wider perceptions of women's role in society. For example, the conservatism of feminism during the inter-war years did little to alter women's domestic image whereas the radical feminist writings of the 1960s and 1970s did provoke more reaction. As a result, women have gained far greater confidence to question their roles in society. But how far has feminism succeeded in giving women a solution to all their concerns? Has not feminism also raised some issues, such as achieving a satisfactory balance between home and work responsibilities, which have yet to be satisfactorily resolved for large numbers of women?

g) Conclusion

At the end of the century, the longevity of female monarchs is again much in evidence. Victoria's great, great granddaughter, Elizabeth II, has reigned since 1952 and, like her predecessor, has witnessed the dramatic changes of a new technological age. The impact of steam power transformed the nineteenth century; the microchip has revolutionised the twentieth century. For women, the most significant differences in 2000, compared with 1900, have been the opportunity to participate in politics, to exercise economic independence and to feel that their status within a community, whether at national or local level, is based on respect and recognition of them as men's equals.

Yet can women afford to be complacent about their achievements?

Is there not a pattern of success and failure underlying much that has affected women during the last hundred years? The suffragettes and suffragists conducted an emotional and determined campaign for the vote yet were forced to compromise. Advocates of equal rights saw their efforts weakened by an acceptance of welfare feminism. During the two World Wars, women seemed to acquire new levels of freedom and responsibilities only to experience a revival of more traditional attitudes in peacetime. Even the 1960s, decade of 'sexual liberation', brought mixed success to women in that many felt that radical left-wing politics showed little understanding of women's issues. The Women's Liberation Movement appeared to herald a new era of emancipation for women, but even that was deflected by a revival of right-wing politics in the 1980s. As we enter, therefore, the twenty-first century, it is important to retain a balanced perspective on past, present and future. The twentieth century was a period which inaugurated far-reaching change for women but yet to be resolved is the issue of how women will ultimately take up their rightful place in British society. If, by the end of the twenty-first century, the subject of 'women' has become redundant, then this question will have been answered.

Working on Chapter 8

Your main task is to prepare guideline notes which might help you to answer broad, synoptic questions on women in twentieth-century Britain. You should now use your notes on this chapter and the themes discussed as the basis for a revision of the whole book. Take each theme in turn and check each chapter to find the relevant evaluation. Keep your assessment simple by dividing up your notes under different headings, e.g. change, continuity, cause, effect, advances, setbacks. You should appreciate that questions which cover change over a long period of time such as one hundred years will not necessarily require a large amount of detailed facts. What will be looked for is an ability to understand the reasons for, and the consequences of, significant changes and to demonstrate an ability to link up different causal factors. When you have finished these key notes, you might want to see whether you could answer a question such as 'Were women significantly better off in 2000 than in 1900'?

Answering essay questions on Chapter 8

1. Discuss the view that the two World Wars only had a short-term impact on the nature of women's employment in Britain.
2. According to socialist feminists in the 1970s, women were the economic victims of capitalism during the twentieth century. Do you agree?

3. To what extent had women's economic status within British society changed by the end of the twentieth century?

4. How far did government legislation determine the role of women within the family between 1918 and 2000?

5. How did attitudes towards marriage change during the course of the twentieth century?

6. To what extent were women more socially independent by 2000?

7. Why have women in Britain failed to gain complete political equality with men?

8. How far did equal suffrage change women's political status in Britain?

9. 'Technological progress in Britain has done little to improve the lives of women.' Do you agree?

10. How significant were educational policies in shaping attitudes towards women between 1918 and 2000?

11. 'Educational reforms after 1945 were an essential prerequisite to the emancipation of women'. Discuss.

12. Assess the view that between 1918 and 1968 the feminist movement achieved little for women.

13. Why was the feminist movement in Britain so often divided during the twentieth century?

14. To what extent had women gained emancipation by 2000?

Hints and advice: With all these questions, the most important starting point is to do an essay plan. These are broad questions so you must be careful that you do not over-emphasise one key idea at the expense of ignoring a number of smaller ones. You must aim for a balanced answer, hence the need to plan your ideas in advance. Map out, either in the form of a diagram or in note form, the main points which you wish to include. Make sure that these subjects will link together and that they will help to support an overall argument. Finally, check that you appreciate what type of question you are answering such as 'why?', 'to what extent?' or 'assess the view that'. As you develop your essay, it will be crucial that you demonstrate how your points are relevant to answering that particular question.

The most difficult challenge in any synoptic question will be to maintain a broad outline whilst not falling into the trap of making too many generalisations. Specific evidence will have to be deployed skilfully as a means of demonstrating a point without indulging in too lengthy discussion. You might find that you have to refer to several pieces of key evidence quite briefly but then draw a general conclusion from that evaluation, explaining its significance in relation to the question. Remember, too, the essay needs to demonstrate a balanced approach, one in which different opinions are carefully evaluated, or different causal factors linked and analysed. Finally, in your conclusion, make sure that you return to your overall assessment, making a clear reference to the question as you bring your essay to a close.

Further Reading

In the last thirty years, a large number of books have been published as a result of the upsurge of interest in women's history. There is a wide-ranging choice of subjects, so it is best to commence with a general book before undertaking more detailed, topic-based study.

1 General Books

Few books provide a general analysis of women's history throughout the whole of the twentieth century. Two useful starting points would be **Martin Pugh**, *Women and the Women's Movement, 1914–1959* (Macmillan, 1992) and **Sue Bruley**, *Women in Britain Since 1900* (Macmillan, 1999). Pugh's book is very detailed but is particularly excellent for its evaluation of inter-war politics and the so-called 'domesticity' of women. Bruley provides a valuable analysis of the whole century, focusing mainly on social and economic issues, although political change is also investigated. **Jane Lewis** has published two books, *Women in England 1870–1950* (Wheatsheaf Books, Ltd., 1984) and *Women in Britain since 1945* (Blackwell, 1992) which both provide valuable analysis of topics such as women's work, the family, class differences, sexual divisions within society. Two useful reference books are **David Butler**, *British Political Facts 1900–1994* (Macmillan, 1994) and **A.H. Halsey** with **Josephine Webb**, eds., *Twentieth-Century British Social Trends* (Macmillan, 2000). Halsey contains a huge range of information such as trends in population, the family, education, health and employment.

2 The World Wars

One approach to understanding women's roles during the World Wars is to read one of the many books written about life on the Home Front. Two books written by **Norman Longmat**e, *How We Lived Then* (Hutchinson & Co., Ltd., 1971) and (ed) *The Home Front* (Chatto & Windus, 1981) contain detailed insights into how the 1939–45 war affected people at home. Both *The Home Front* and **Dorothy Sheridan**'s, ed., *Wartime Women* (Heinemann, 1990) have a fascinating anthology of women's recollections of wartime experiences. Two excellent texts are **Penny Summerfield**'s, *Women Workers in the Second World War* (Croom Helm, 1984) and **Gail Braybon** and **Penny Summerfield**'s, *Out of the Cage: Women's Experiences in Two World Wars* (Pandora, 1987). Both are invaluable for their wide-ranging analysis of women's work. There are fewer books specialising in the First World War, but **Gail Braybon**'s *Women Workers in the First World War* (Croom Helm, 1981) and **Deborah Thom**'s *Nice Girls and Rude Girls: Women Workers in World War I* (I.B. Tauris, 1998) would both make essential reading.

3 Women's Political History

Many books have been written about the suffrage movement, especially on the years prior to 1914, but historians have tended to show less interest in women's political progress after 1928. In the *Access to History* series, **Paula Bartley**'s *Votes for Women 1860–1928* (Hodder and Stoughton, 1998) deals very thoroughly with all aspects of the suffrage campaign. **Harold L. Smith**'s *The British Women's Suffrage Campaign 1866–1928* (Longman, 1998) is likewise a succinct but scholarly synthesis of the suffrage movement, with both a collection of documents and detailed bibliography. Smith's book, plus that of **Sandra Stanley Holton**, *Feminism and Democracy: Women's Suffrage and Reform Politics in Britain 1900–1918* (Cambridge University Press, 1986), also seeks to place the suffrage movement within a wider political context. On the anti-suffragists, **Brian Harrison**'s *Separate Spheres: The Opposition to Women's Suffrage in Britain, 1890–1920* (Croom Helm, 1978) was the first book to investigate the extent of suffrage opposition. **Cheryl Law**'s *Suffrage and Power: The Women's Movement 1918–1928* (I.B. Tauris, 1997) provides a stimulating interpretation of the suffrage movement after 1918 arguing that there was continuity, as opposed to partial collapse, within the women's movement throughout the 1920s. **Johanna Alberti**'s *Beyond Suffrage* (Macmillan, 1989) is equally sympathetic to this view and, like Law, considers the contributions made by different women's groups as well as politicians to the campaign for equal suffrage. Several books examine women's parliamentary role – **Melville Currell**, *Political Woman* (Croom Helm, 1974), **Elizabeth Vallance**, *Women in the House* (Athlone, 1979), **Pamela Brookes**, *Women at Westminster* (Peter Davies, 1967), **Melanie Phillips**, *The Divided House: Westminster* (Sidgwick & Jackson, 1980), **April Carter**, *The Politics of Women's Rights* (Longman, 1988) all give a range of insights into the successes and failures of women in politics after 1928.

4 Women's Social and Economic History

Elizabeth Roberts', *Women's Work 1840–1940* (Cambridge University Press, 1995) is a very accessible, concise study of the issues relating to women's work and as such is a useful introduction to the subject. **Carol Dyhouse**'s, *Feminism and the Family in England, 1880–1939* (Blackwell, 1989) is equally useful for the interwar years, especially as she includes some critique of differing feminist ideas towards women and the family. As the title suggests, **Deidre Beddoe**'s, *Back to Home and Duty: Women Between the Wars, 1918-1939* (Pandora, 1989) examines the economic and social trends affecting women after 1918. The two studies by **Viola Klein**, *Britain's Married Women Workers* (Routledge and Kegan Paul, 1965) and **Alva Myrdal** and **Viola Klein**, *Women's Two Roles Home and Work* (Routledge and Kegan Paul, 1956), based on surveys of women's work in the 1950s and 1960s, provide the first contemporary re-evaluation of women's economic status in the post-1945 period. **Elizabeth Wilson**'s, *Only Half-Way to Paradise Women in Postwar Britain: 1945–1968* (Tavistock Publications, 1980) contains a broad-ranging analysis of women's changing economic and social circumstances after 1945 as well as examining the roots of the Women's Liberation Movement.

5 Feminism

Although **Barbara Caine**'s, *English Feminism 1780–1980* (Oxford University Press, 1997) covers two centuries, it is helpful to have the contextual background of feminism in the late eighteenth and nineteenth centuries explained as a prelude to understanding feminism in the twentieth century. Caine successfully places the feminist movement within a broader political, social and economic framework. Similar insights are offered by **Harold L. Smith**, ed., *British Feminism in the Twentieth Century* (Edward Elgar, 1990) and **Olive Banks**, *Faces of Feminism: A Study of Feminism as a Social Movement* (Blackwell, 1981). A more in-depth understanding of feminism can also be gained by looking at **Brian Harrison**'s biography of *Prudent Revolutionaries: Portraits of British Feminists between the Wars* (Clarendon Press, 1987). There is a huge range of books written by feminists on women's history, some of the most notable being: **Betty Friedan**, *The Feminine Mystique* (Penguin Books, 1965), **Germaine Greer**, *The Female Eunuch* (Flamingo, 1971), Kate Millett, *Sexual Politics* (Abacus, 1972), **Sheila Rowbotham**, *The Past is Before Us: Feminism in Action since the 1960s* (Pandora, 1989) and *A Century of Women* (Penguin Books, 1999), **Beatrix Campbell** and **Anna Coote**, *Sweet Freedom: The Struggle for Women's Liberation* (Blackwell, 1987), and **Jill Liddington**, *The Long Road to Greenham: Feminism and Antimilitarism in Britain since 1820* (Virago, 1989). All these books were landmark publications in that they each offered new, challenging interpretations on aspects of the women's movement and corresponding ideas.

6 Autobiographies, Biographies, Diaries and Letters

As interest in women's history proliferated so did the number of publications by, or of, women. **Hannah Mitchell**'s experiences as an early working-class socialist and feminist are graphically retold in *The Hard Way Up* (Virago, 1977) whilst a more middle-class observation of life as an independent woman can be found in **Vera Brittain**'s, *Testament of Youth* (Gollancz, 1933) and *Testament of Experience* (Gollancz, 1953). **Edith Summerskill**'s, *A Woman's World* (Heinemann, 1967), **Margaret Bondfield**'s, *A Life's Work* (Hutchinson, 1948) and **Patricia Hollis**' biography of the pioneer socialist MP *Jennie Lee: A Life* (Oxford University Press, 1997) are three very individual accounts of the challenges facing women who entered politics. For two more recent records of life in Westminster, **Barbara Castle**'s, *The Castle Diaries 1974–76* (Weidenfeld and Nicolson, 1980) and **Margaret Thatcher**'s *The Path to Power* (HarperCollins, 1995) and *The Downing Street Years* (HarperCollins, 1993) reflect the opinions of two of Britain's very prominent female politicians.

Index